JEEPERS AND CRIMINY!
Are You Following This?

A Helpful If Inexact Proletarian/Smart
Ars Poetic Manifesto

JEEPERS AND CRIMINY!
Are You Following This?

A Helpful If Inexact Proletarian/Smart
Ars Poetic Manifesto

Frank Rogaczewski

American Letters & Commentary, Inc.

Jeepers And Criminy! Are You Following This?
A Helpful If Inexact Proletarian/Smart Ars Poetic Manifesto

ISBN 10: 0-9825647-9-0
ISBN 13: 978-0-9825647-9-0

Cover Image by Westend61/Getty Images
Book Design by David Ray Vance

American Letters & Commentary, Inc.
PO Box # 830365
San Antonio, TX 78283

www.amletters.org

In Memory of
Catherine Kasper

Contents

Resurrection of the Great American Elegy   *9*

How Economics Became a Discipline   *14*

Enlightened Capitalism Frees the Slaves!   *20*

"Don't Vote, Vomit"   *24*

At the Impromptu Surrealists Convention   *27*

Sputnik and the Russian Bear   *31*

Seven Deadlies: A Prose Sestina   *35*

Is This a Bad Time?   *45*

"Stone Free"?   *57*

Amazing Scientific Breakthrough: Poem =Orgone Accumulator!   *62*

We Each Fertilize Our Own Straw Bale   *76*

Just Like *Volume Two*   *81*

Mark Rothko's Subway   *86*

Certain Curious Proclivities Abide Amidst the Post-Bride Mountainside Laboratory-Hideaway   *88*

Theodicy   *91*

Armed Teachers [with Mental Illness]   *93*

Search Me, Little Varmints   *99*

The Great American Jesus   *104*

Toward Smart-Ass Proletarian Poetry   *107*

Notes   *123*

Resurrection of the Great American Elegy

Just like vampires, the neighborhood agents of Cthulhu cannot abide a good dog. I'd walk Sammy, and the howls and screeches, the hackles raised and cackles broken, the withering stares. "Oh!" they would complain: "Keep that dog off my lawn!" "You'd damn well better pick up after that dog!" "He raised his leg!!" "Why don't you keep him in your yard?" Yep, they'd be standing right on their front porches practicing their moist and guttural Cthulhu language—*K-too-lhoo Ftaghn!* and all that sort of thing—and Sammy would saunter by and pee on their misshapen Rose of Sharons with the flowers that looked like chihuahua heads. Then I'd have to apologize, and we'd have to hurry along. Sometimes their cephalopod-headed, wiry-tentacled excuses for dogs escaped their yards and attempted attacks on Sammy, who was a sniffer of all and biter of none, so luckily Jasmine arrived after a while to get feisty on his behalf, and I'd no longer have to run him away from the ungainly looking critters. Not to mention the possum and raccoons with human faces, and the rabbits that leapt in unpredictable, non-geometrical, unearthly fashion. In his own endearing way, saving his pee for sniffing here and then appropriately applying there, Sammy exposed ooodles of agents of Cthulhu in our neighborhood. Their grand plan was to transmogrify Berywn, Illinois, into Cthulhuville, complete with the grey front lawns whereupon meteorites from beyond known dimensions of space had fallen and dissolved, the neighborhood church wherein shambling things worked upon the belfry—caution tape bestrooning the street as Sammy, Jasmine, and

I worried by—the house kitty corner from the church with the wide open second story window in the dead of thirteen below zero winter night (mighty reminiscent of H.P. Lovecraft's "Cool Air"), the fabled Starry Wisdom Tavern, and city hall, offices filled with more shambling human-faced grimacing things, building fronted by the red, white, and grey American flag. Even Svengoolie, painted on a garage wall a block east had to go, I figure as an offense to the star-haunting Old Ones. *Not dead enough!* Part of the cosmic conspiracy, of course, to bring down a particular dog-loving, left-wing poet for having exposed their tidy little suburban—not to mention literary—secret many years ago in a poem that started out to describe a simple walk with Sammy Boy. (By the way, isn't it uncanny how when you find a cosmic conspiracy, you are so often right at the center of it?) Hence, like something out of Stephen King's "Jerusalem's Lot" (the early, pre-vampire, Lovecraftian story wherein giant otherworldly worms called *shibbermetimbers* or some such tunnel throughout the town) cult members filled their pre-wormed-out underground tunnels with medical apparatuses and even certain particular and peculiar personnel borrowed from local hospitals in their odious plot to surgically mutilate, physically eviscerate, and psychically rearrange those who might not be predisposed to favor a Chtulhuville—left-wing dog walkers, for instance. A nice young couple two blocks up the street completely disappear—and their little dogs too, Ginsberg and Chomsky. Meanwhile, at Starry Wisdom Tavern the deceased Ralph Ellison's talking to the long-gone Richard Wright about how the latter was the other soul's early influence when suddenly Wright's corpse is inhabited by T.S. Eliot's ghost. The stench of kippers and rotgut whiskey fills the air and a fakey upper crusty British voice comes from Wright's mouth: "The Communist Party in Harlem is nothing but an objective correlative for King Bolo." I'm carried underground and cryosurgically damaged, surgically dismantled, catheterized, fistulized, colostomized, recatheterized, all to the vapid, new-agey chanting of the Harvard Alumni Choir, supposedly innocently caroling the neighborhood, but actually tonally preparing the way for the return of the mad old gods and incidentally once again demonstrating the reason we've never seen Lovecraft's Miskatonic University and Harvard in the same place at the same time. And after each torture I'm crawling back up to the surface—*Not (gasp!) dead (gak!) enough!*—in hopes the demonic nightmare will end. All the while Sammy has been losing his abilities, growing old—for two winters hobbling up the gangway with me, limping ahead off leash toward the front lawn, hoping before it's time to go inside for the pleasures of wholesome neighborhood sniffs of wholesome neighborhood dogs. In the spring when Sammy passes quietly away, the agents of Cthulhu expect that just as with the death of Professor Angell at the opening pages of Lovecraft's "The Call of Cthulhu," the sad leave-taking of the angel dog will be for them a fortuitous sign. Instead the Cthulhu agents have to stay out of sight as the human neighbors ask after Sammy, remember him fondly as a good dog, commiserate. "All you can do is cry," one neighbor says. And Jasmine bravely holds down the fort—though she becomes a bit indiscriminate about just whom she's biting. Yet Robert, Abby's person, defends Jasmine, saying, "She's not trying to hurt most of the other dogs, just those funny headed ones with the tentacles." This is when Beverly and I decide Jasmine needs a new companion, a German shepherd-Australian cattle dog or Catahoula hound or Chow Chow or all of the above mix from a South Dakota American Indian reservation. And you know how it's mentioned in many a Lovecraft story that aboriginal peoples are somehow more aware of the Old Ones? Do you wonder whether it applies to reservation-born dogs? Seamus did give some early indications. He didn't dig up the barren spots in the yard like Sammy did. It was as if he already knew about what happened to those meteorites. He developed a real penchant for chewing on wood—twigs and sticks and even branches—of which we thought nothing for a while, but then strange things began happening. Even though Seamus evinced no curiosity concerning the garage as Sammy always had, the woodpiles began disappearing from there. A few days later, Ron, our neighbor two doors north complained that his gas can had gone missing from his garage: "I can't understand it. The door was locked." Did I ever tell you about the big deal we made when we first discovered Jasmine could unzip backpacks and tents? I only mention it. No particular reason. Beverly and I began hearing that the grouches who'd complained about Sammy now bellyached about being dogbitten in the dead of night. Certainly, our dogs sometimes went out into the yard at 3 a.m. or so, but the yard was gated, and the dogs weren't out there all that long. Then came the late-night fire at the house kitty corner from the church, the reanimated corpse's pained guttural cries from the window wide open to the January air: "*Ka-poo-ie! Ftaghn!*" And from the belfry of the church flew thousands of fist-sized, bat-winged batrachian possumish and raccoonish things, darkening the already moonless sky. Meanwhile, Starry Wisdom Tavern in flames, the dead Confederates amongst the crowd are singing "The Night They Drove Old Dixie Down." And from Ellison's own mouth the bad bourbon stench and the fakey upper crust British of Eliot, "It appears our nightly debauch ends not with a whang but with a pimple." And the bar proceeds to clear out, as in "Hurry Up" and all that rot. Rumors fly that a few of the Confederates and local agents of Cthulhu, bitten by a couple of dogs, have bubbled and melted down like Wilbur Whateley in "The Dunwich Horror" into noisome and garish stains on the sidewalk. I'm out in the yard calling the dogs and I notice a few agents of Cthulhu out in their own yards chanting, "Nobody loves us! Everybody hates us! We're Out in the Garden to Eat Some Worms!" In this neighborhood, that's quite a meal. I still can't locate those dogs, so I go back into the house for treats, and what do you know? They're both lounging comfortably on the living room couch, only the mildest scent of burning kindling about them, and Seamus is chomping on some nasty little winged thing I don't even think of taking from him. "Good dogs," I say, and now I'm out in the snow, walking Sammy toward the el stop to meet Beverly, not an anti-dog complaint to be heard from here to the Eisenhower, and he will soon see her approaching from the station and rush forward and leap up to greet her.

How Economics Became a Discipline

Barter is first established so that the person who has an abundance of yak milk can trade x quantity of said milk for y quantity of Zenith color TVs—"The quality goes in before the name goes on." Everything moves along as if on a conveyer belt through all those barbarous and feudal times, and here and there a medium is found or invented via means of which exchange may be expanded, x amount of quality (in slave hours or serf hours or artisan hours or eunuch hours or some such) going in before the rich get richer. Maybe the first medium of exchange were sea shells, but when she starts selling them down by the shore, we switch to gold and silver. Soon explorers sail out and bring back spices, gold, silver, jewels, and, of course, slaves. Right on time, here come Columbus's ships: the *Nina*, the *Pinta,* and the *Santa Variola.* The filthy, creepy, scurvy and smallpox and syphilis-ridden sailors on these ships see the happy, beautiful people on the shore, and the first thought that occurs to them, of course, "Let's make them our slaves." (It is very difficult to get those slave hours of quality if you don't have the slaves to put in the hours.) In Jolly Olde England the precursor to our ideal of the mansion on the hill above all the farmers in the dell is one where the would-be farmers are peasants on measly, coffin-sized plots of land eking out a bare subsistence before being thrown off said measle and proletarianized. Meanwhile the trade of one commodity for another by means of the medium of money (or lucre, from the Latin *lucrum*, meaning "material gain or profit") expressed in a formula as C–M–C shifts over to the use of money to create more money (or "filthy lucre") expressed M-C-M' wherein the medium becomes the end, and the process of primitive accumulation of capital (or *loot* from the Hindi *lut*, meaning *rob)* is unending, unrelenting, uncanny. Even when the ex-slaves escape from the stale hell of the South they find the fresh hell of the North. "Give me your tired, your poor,/ Your huddled masses yearning to breathe free,/ And I'll grind their bones to make my bread." By this time moral philosophy has given birth to economics, as Adam Smith attempts to contrive a logical path from the conundrum whereby the grubby, sleazy self-interest of a veritable rabble of individual capitalists may somehow make for a society cooperative enough to keep a nation from falling backward into hunting and gathering, dueling and tobacco drooling, or oligarchifying and uglifying. Speaking of nostalgia for the South, what crazy white folks arguing about "reverse discrimination" are trying to say—that is, the logical construction in post-syllogistic and relatively uncomplicated form—is as follows: "I'm like rubber and you're like glue. Whatever *racist* you call me bounces off me and sticks to you." Yessiree, those Southern plantation—meaning slave labor camp—owners, they had time to sit around and philosophize, create logical paths and constructions from conundrums: "Let's see, mansion on the hill, cotton fields below, slaves under the lash, and where did that Nat Turner go off to and why are all my neighbors' houses burning?" This, and the general European rape and pillage of Africa, Asia and the Americas occurs at just the moment when moral philosophy begets aesthetics in order that formal gardens with manicured hedges and myriad topiary pillars and balls, fountains and walkways may gentle the spirits of the slave-drivers, oligarchs and corporate CEOs. You can't throw a rotten apple without hitting one of the landscape painters all over the landscape. And if you're a peasant trying to eke out an existence on any of said landscapes once they've been enclosed, you'll be hanged by the neck until dead and your body given over to some medical college. Now we're off to the company town where *The Dearborn Independent* arrives with the latest installment of the Henry Ford-inspired "The International Jew." But while the Social Darwinists march around in their Klan outfits and cabinet posts, Charlie himself hangs out in the Galapagos in order to undermine slavery by declining hierarchy within species. Jesus may've said the poor will always be with you, but not when you're young at heart. Meanwhile, the discovery of labor power, which, invested in commodities gives them their use value and their exchange value. This is easy enough to understand: you'd like to buy some marijuana (assuming that we're in Denver or on Venice Beach or over in Amsterdam [watch out for the bikes!!!]). Now, use value is the recreational or medical benefit you would derive from these marijuana cigarettes, but you need to pay their exchange value, which at its most basic (before taxes and all—refer to *loot* above) is the labor power invested in growing the weed, acquiring the papers, rolling the joints, and packaging the product (especially the plastic wrap over the package itself—we already have a plastic tumor the size of Texas in the Pacific along with the radioactive fish [which may or may not kill the tapeworms they carry], fracking all over the nation [not to mention leaky oil pipelines], and hunters creeping into bear dens to shoot the cubs. Makes me feel pretty grizzly just thinking about that list of environmental legislative skullduggery and corporate sliminess and depredations) or, as Marx would say—are you following this? Economics is not only about genetic algorithms and valuation and game theory, you know—the commodity. One thing about labor power that Karl Marx commented on back in the day is that what the corporate and other elite actually buy is the ability to labor, and what they get is labor power invested in commodities, which is the only exchange in which, everything else being equal, this one is never equal. The capitalist always wins. That's why they call it capitalism and not proletarianism, or these days, precariatism. But the other thing about labor power is that it's transmogrified human creativity. So Nat Turner's labor power may invest the cotton he gathers under the whip with value, but Nat Turner's labor power outside of the societally-imposed workday takes the form of human creativity, allows him to preach the Bible in the most original ways and allows him to lead a slave revolt, which would be a revolt against the Original Sin of the nation. We are told, by the way, that *precariat* is a portmanteau word combining *precarious* with *proletariat*. But wait, you inquire, what do slave revolts and tapeworms in salmon and syphilis-ridden sailors and portmanteaus have to do with economics becoming a discipline? I can tell you that Adam Smith solved his conundrum with nothing up his sleeve but the invisible hand, the shadow of divine intelligence that Darwin banished by mere chance. Jesus said the poor will always be with you, but the Statue of Liberty said, "Give me your tired, your poor,/Your muddled asses writing poetry." ("Honey, I'm home!") Or, regarding Nat Turner, and the rest of us too for that matter, it might could be the other way around, that human creativity under the domination of the market is bartered, disciplined, and transmogrified into labor power at the capitalist's pleasure for the capitalist's leisure. Add financialization with all its loan ratings, derivatives, foreign exchange swaps, futures markets, hedge funds, collateralized debt obligations, and—as they put it at Wells Fargo in real classy economics-as-a-discipline jargon—"ghetto loans" for "mud people"—and we've got one helluva discombobulation of a nation. Or maybe you're in Nicaragua and right-wing as all get-out and want to buy guns and ammunition and bombs and missiles and all kinds of firepower to overthrow a democratically-elected government. Meanwhile, the CIA notices you've got plenty of cocaine they would like to exchange for the benefit of the Crips and Bloods and the War on Drugs. Pretty soon you Contras are up to your ears in guns and money. And drug lords got their crack and their greenbacks. Meanwhile, Black neighborhoods have got crack up to their neighbors' ears and police and SWAT teams and mandatory minimums and three strikes you got life and if not life then a felony charge that sticks like super glue. *Prison industry stocks up 100% since Trump win!* Prison being where capital and punishment meet! We're living in an oligarchy's aesthetic of economic bondage and discipline, wherein the prison as Enlightenment project transmogrifies and multiplies as myriad panoptikants. Then there's neoliberal economic theory: forty-something years of class war by the elite on the rest of us, more and more of us joining the precariat so that we have to give up the *portmanteau* part of the expression *portmanteau word* and settle for *backpack word* or maybe even *extra-hefty garbage bag word*. And this economic situation obtains even though *panoptikant* as portmanteau word combines Jeremy

Bentham's ideal and unrealizable institutional design whereby all (*pan-*) prisoners in a given prison may be observed (*-opti-*) by a single keeper without the prisoners being able to tell they are being watched, with Immanuel Kant (*-kant*), the philosopher who gave us the thing-in-itself, which we may never know—I hope you're keeping up now; this is no time for lollygagging in game theory or bartering apples for tomatoes with which to brain the landscape painters—hence, we bring together the unknowable and the unrealizable, in the neoliberal capitalist negation of the negation of negation, investing all our tomorrows with unaffordability, unacceptability, and, most certainly, unexchangeability.

Enlightened Capitalism Frees the Slaves!

Here we are, 1888, St. Louis, Missouri, inside the Pearl Milling Company where the workers are exploited and covered with flour dust. The owners, Chris L. Rutt and Charles G. Underwood, notice that their workers look to be wearing whiten face, which may have been behind the original inspiration for Aunt Jemima, if it wasn't a trip to the local minstrel show and a listen to the song "Old Aunt Jemima." Yes, gone are the days. In any case, the actor playing Aunt Jemima wore an apron and kerchief, which outfit she "liberated," but not with the character, who nevertheless remained obliged to promote products of the Pearl Milling Company, which was sold to the Davis Milling Company in 1890, Aunt Jemima being sold as part of the lot. I almost wrote *Mulling* rather than *Milling*, and certainly there would be a different kind of exploitation going on in a Mulling Company: "C'mon, you bastards, I don't hire you to sit around talking. Think it over!!" Soon the jobs are outsourced to India, Pakistan, South Korea and elsewheres where think is cheap. By the way, speaking of enlightened capitalism, you don't generally hear of an oil drilling company with a corrupting blot on their record. The corrupting blot's usually all over the Gulf of Mexico or Prince William Sound, Alaska, or pretty soon first thing people see when coming to the U.S. from Europe will be the Statue and Great Stain of Liberty. Perhaps the Goddess of Liberty herself would be draped in the Great Stain. This would keep her warm in the winter, and also appropriately covered so that no fundamentalist Christian politician need be concerned that while he stood before her during some commercial spot, Liberty would pull a wardrobe malfunction. Meanwhile, a long time before Janet Jackson's flashy scene, an ex-slave named Nancy Green was hired as a spokesperson for the Aunt Jemima pancake mix. She even made an appearance at the 1893 World's Columbian Exposition in Chicago, Illinois, to make pancakes. This, we imagine, was a real high point in her career. The Aunt Jemima marketing slogan was, "I'se in town, honey." But she wasn't for all that long, being sold up the river to Quaker Oats Company in 1926. Sold, I almost said, by the Davis *Mauling* Company. And I don't mean shopping. Imagine the exploitation that'd go on in a mauling company. Why, it would be a slaughterhouse. And here we are, 1966, Quaker introduces syrup under the slogan, "Aunt Jemima, what took you so long?" Aunt Jemima may not say much in response, but here it is, 1966, one hundred years after slavery was supposed to have been over and Black people are still fighting for basic civil rights. "And you crazy white folks come up with a slogan where *you* are asking *me* what's taking so long? What is the matter with you crazy people? Don't have the sense God gave a mule. Maybe a shark though. Whole buncha sharks. Madison Avenue and Wall Street toothy kinda sharks, too." By now you're beginning to wonder how it is we're going to find out how enlightened capitalism freed the slaves in a prose poem that begins in 1888, which would be a bit beyond *in media res*, if you follow my meaning. Of course, one can always begin beyond or even in *in media res* rather than way back in *ab ovo*, or "from the egg"–which is a reference to a Horatian idea that one likes to have breakfast before setting out on a long narrative or an epic poem or some such—and then one can easily recount earlier events through use of the "flashback" or *analepsis*—which sounds like something systemic and inflammatory, but that's only in the case of stories with a lot of contention and hard feelings; kidnappings of women or fake insults to women, wars and civil wars and redemptions; Satan's temptations, bar fights, cursings, gnashing of broken teeth and would-be nations, and mutterings under the breath. It's a good thing I didn't mention a Davis *Molling* Company, because, truth to tell, I don't know how you'd keep such a company staffed, what with the gun molls always running off with their wiseguy fellas on bank robberies and other escapades. And where do you get foremen to supervise a bunch of women with Tommy guns? You better believe the plantation overseers would've thought twice about taking those jobs if all the slaves were similarly mollified. Perhaps this explains why enlightened capitalism doesn't want to free the slaves right in the middle of slavery. Also, emancipation's pretty controversial, and enlightened capitalism is more interested in going with the flow, so to speak, you know, like where the money is. Unless, of course, not enough money *is*. So enlightened capitalism would probably rather start *ab ovo*, and have a nice breakfast first—Aunt Jemima pancakes and syrup. Then enlightened capitalism will take us over to Uncle Ben's website. Yes, that's the Uncle Ben on the rice packages with the recipes and all. Did you know that back in the old days before enlightened capitalism freed the slaves, white folks addressed older Black men as "Uncle" because they couldn't bring themselves to address them as "Sir"? You've heard of field slaves and house slaves. Today Uncle Ben is chairman of the board slave. As is, he's virtual chairman of the board. This is how enlightened capitalism, with the aid of the internet, is solving all the problems of the world. The internet, by the way, began as a military project, but today anyone can get on the world wide web and find pictures from the latest despoliations and depredations of globalization: Sludge birds; black waves and browncaps; stain on the sea twice the size of Maryland and heading for the coast; radioactive fish all over the Pacific. I might've said the Davis *Moiling* Company because whatever mulling or milling or mauling used to go on in there, it was way discombobulating and too close to the shoreline. Maybe you'd rather just eat your pancakes and set out for closure before there's some sort of flashback to Reconstruction times, when enlightened capitalism thought to itself, How can we get those downright systemic and inflammatory abolitionists to put a cork in it?

"Don't Vote, Vomit"

My yoga therapist asks me if I think we can change the world by thought, so the thought occurs that there are physicists who believe quantum mechanics are at work not only on the subatomic level but on our own supposedly Newtonian one as well. They have even conducted experiments with creating tapes by computer, randomizing sound so that what comes from right and left speaker is, statistically speaking, liable to even out over time. Then the unheard tapes are given to volunteers who are asked to think the sound occurs more on the right side than the left, and the tapes, replayed, work exactly that way, contrary to statistics, to contemporary physics, to Newton, and suggesting that the world is awash with subatomic particles that we observe into the stable objects of the world—plants and birds and rocks and IKEA coffee tables and bookshelves (well, kinda stable) flora and fauna, and ourselves (oh, we're holding on for dear stability's sake) and others (ditto). Problem is: if the first observers transformed—or first formed—the objects of the world, did they also fashion forever the relations between objects, between people, between animals and people? The power relations? The greed? Which brings us to the film about Phil Ochs in which a demonstrator outside the '68 Democratic Convention holds up a sign that reads as does the title of this poem. Just think: the first inauguration of Dubya, protesters cordoned off, and waves of vomit come rolling down Pennsylvania Avenue, carry away the presidential limo, and wash it into the now-stenchy Potomac, stenchy with vomit *and* unelected president. Or think: Ronald Reagan shows up in Philadephia, Mississippi, where three civil rights workers—Michael Schwerner, James Chaney, Andrew Goodman—were murdered by a sheriff's office/Klan alliance in 1964, and just as Reagan opens his mouth to speak of states' rights and kick off his presidential campaign—a miracle! Half-digested jelly beans vomit down from the sky! In the experiment with the once-randomized, tape-recorded sounds, it's as if the volunteers thought their way back in time to when the tapes were first recorded. Or it's as if time has no meaning when our world acts according to quantum mechanical principles. Just think: Ronald Reagan's entire right-wing presidential campaign rained out by vomit. Or the great Clinton-Trump debate, with Trump trying to stalk around Hillary as he slips and slides and flops on his bulbous backside in the regurgitation of the spectators, and Hillary Clinton trying to distance herself from her previous conjurations of African American pre-teen "super-predators" over the sound of generations of lesser-evil voters just spewing forth—the sound trumpeting Trump away, leaving Clinton speechless, standing there with chunks of yup-chuck (yes, the vomit of yuppies) in her hair. Can we change the world by vomit? Just think: Willie Horton ads washed away in the flood, as are Barry Goldwater, Richard Nixon, Gerald Ford, Bill Clinton, Donald Trump, Jeff Sessions, Betsy DeVos, and the whole Trump Klan. Wash away mass incarceration, trickle-down economics, secret and not-so-secret wars (against Nicaragua, against Iraq, against Syria, Libya and Yemen) and fraudulent wars (against drugs and against cancer). Just think: the whole economics department at the University of Chicago flushed out into Lake Michigan in about 1970. Just think: a socialist Chile in the 21ˢᵗCentury, a socialist Europe, a socialist Iraq, Syria, Yemen, Somalia—nation after nation, a Domino Theory event resulting from too many folks ingesting those Domino's Pizzas. Yes, and think about it: neoliberalism washed away on a veritable tsunami of vomit while the Eugene Debs/Emma Goldman bloc takes the White House and hires union labor to paint it red and black.

At the Impromptu Surrealists Convention

It's almost his turn so he'd better think of something surrealist pretty quick. I know, he thinks, *bats in the belfry*. Oh, but that's a cliché. But aren't clichés often phrases or expressions that once were surrealist but simply have lost their once-surrealist edge? Their dreamlike *je ne sais qua*? And how to restore that evanescent quality? Perhaps *vampire bats in the belfry*. No, that's gothic. True, but one could argue that the surreal is haunted by the gothic. Of course, that would be using logical reasoning, and you can't just stand up at an Impromptu Surrealists Convention and start blabbering logical reasoning. Meanwhile, you're wondering: Why the *Impromptu* Surrealists? Why not the *Spur-of-the-Moment* Surrealists? Or perhaps the *Unprepared* Surrealists? Well, you'd have to admit, *Unprepared* might evoke just the hint of a suggestion of an ethos quite contrary to the spirit of the convention. Maybe *rabid bats in the . . .* No, whatever else that one might be, it's too realist. It'll set people to thinking about the possibility of bats in the convention hall. Bat aspiration and rabies. It'll give people nightmares. Years of therapy. "It's because as a young child, doctor, I saw my parents in bed with a bear." "And so you fear bats?" "Yes, I'm a surrealist." "If that's so, I'm sure you'll be able to tell me how many surrealists it takes to screw in a light bulb." "Why, as many as would ever dream of fitting on the beds and futons inside." And wasn't Ferdinand castigated last year for the realism of his impromptu "At the Surrealist Funeral Home the Crowd at the Wake Play 'Exquisite Corpse'"? Perhaps you'd rather the *Unscripted* Surrealists Convention? Yes, but then you do lose the musical connotation with *Impromptu*. Sweat beads begin to form upon his forehead as his time grows nearer. Holy Mother Magritte! This feels as of the approach of death itself. Yes, Death in the shape of a beautiful woman in a wedding dress and wearing pearls of wisdom about her throat, but her face, her face is the very shape and form of . . . No, the woman with the face of Henry VIII has been done before, by someone in the French section of the Impromptu Surrealists International. Have I mentioned the rumor that many of the male Surrealists failed to wash their hands when exiting the Men's room? We might be tempted to call this the *Unsanitary* Surrealists Convention. Yes, the English section claims handwashing failures were excessive and almost exclusively on the part of the French. "Don't they realize that's why we call syphilis the French disease?" "I heard it was the Spanish disease," says the Dutch Surrealist. "It's the Polish disease," says the Russian. Suddenly we are reminded of the fate of the Second International during World War I, when most national sections betrayed their internationalist principles and supported their own ruling classes. What were they dreaming? Lenin and Luxemburg washed their hands of them. And who do you think appears in surrealist literary texts more frequently, Lenin or Freud? Oh, let's face facts (such as we may be dreaming them), it would have to be Freud, but often he comes in the form of a beautiful woman, but her face, her face gives people mid-day nightmares. Years of off-the-cuff commentary on the unnatural nature of capitalist society. And myth. And the myth of capitalist growth. Let's not forget post-Medusan commentary on overcompensation for penis envy. But, of course, neither totems nor taboos are entirely appropriate here, and he's moments away from his moment, and he wishes he could refrain from thinking about bats, but his mind will go nowhere but bats. Perhaps if he runs off to the Men's room. But no, the French surrealists will be putting on a show of handwashing in order to avoid blame for what they call "the English disease." Besides, the stalls will all be occupied by surrealists on their cell phones mining friends and relatives for supposedly impromptu material by inquiring after their dreams. He knows the whole convention is all show—a sham, a farce, a charade. And yet, *bat wings on baseball bats*? No, that's a cartoon! He's so nervous! Sweat drips from places sweat drips from. Then he stands, raises his arm in what these days might be called a Hitler salute but was once the proper approach to the American flag (before Hitler, that is) (and before those deodorant commercials with all those underarm perspirations, stains, and exasperations), and enunciates: "I pledge allegiance to the bats of the United States of America, and to the stalactites from which they hang, one nation, under bats, with flea bites and rabies for all." By the time he's done, he looks a bit like Leon Trotsky. Someone looking quite a bit like Trotsky's one-time friend Bukharin asks, "What about 'under God'? Shouldn't our bats be 'under God'? Or *En guarde?*" The crowd goes crazy. *"EN GUARDE!!!"* *"TRES, MUCHO, SEHR, VERY, PROPRIO POLITICO!"* They put him on their shoulders. The crowd goes askew. They carry him into the Men's room and wash their hands while he washes his. It goes without saying that evocations of locations and nations of syphilis are being contained, controlled and countermanded. And they look into the mirrors above the sinks, to their faces, their hair, Oh, Medusa, what took you so long? And they all have pancakes and waffles all over America. North and south of the Mason-Dixon line. Until someone asks, Wasn't the Hitler salute more nostalgic than surreal? Only in America. Then someone explodes, "I knew syphilis was the American disease," and pieces of him land on people's heads and shoulders, on the tables stacked with convention literature, and on the consumables for the surrealist bake sale. The convention fractures into factions calling one another "Sham" and "Charade," using their cell phones to find French, Spanish, Russian, Lithuanian, Creole, Albanian, English, Esperanto, and other translations for these insults. The Turkish section raises a banner: "Syphilis is the Christian Disease!" The sky darkens with rabid bats, militantly gothic, hovering over the convention center, threatening like an unnatural tornado of economic devastation. Perhaps next year this will all be forgotten at the Extemporaneous Surrealists Convention. Perhaps not. The bats descend.

Sputnik and the Russian Bear

for Karen and Bill Couch, and for Mom

So the dang bear bends down the pole upon which the birdfeeder sits and helps himself to what were supposed to be bird treats. "Pokey Bottom," they call him—*they* being my mother Louise, sister Karen, and brother-in-law Bill. Karen sends pictures of the neighborhood bear from Barronett, Wisconsin, where she and Bill live, just a country mile or so from my mother. No, this is not the great Russian bear from Joseph McCarthy's gin and tonics— fearsome Soviet bear with a Stalin mustache and proclivity for world conquest. Really, this furry fellow just wants that peanut butter and birdseed sandwich, suet, grape jelly, and whatever you folks got in your garbage. In the middle of the night. Banging around out there in the dark. Barronett, Wisconsin. And where did you say is the next stoplight? Any light? So, then Karen sends me a *Guardian* article about hungry Russian bears digging up human corpses since cemeteries "offer a 'refrigerator'-like supply of easy food." I see Yogi and Boo Boo some distance from Jellystone Park digging up their pic-a-nic baskets: "Gee, Yogi, this one looks like Ranger Smith." And I can understand why Sputnik, Karen and Bill's feisty cairn terrier, barks his little head off from the safety of the living room window sill every time that flea-bitten, fulla-peanut-butter-and-birdseed bear ventures near. The Russian bear image actually goes back to Tsarist times, wherein you might find sagacious political cartoons of said bear outmaneuvering the British lion in Central Asia by—get this metaphor for strategic advantage—sitting on the Persian cat. Ouch! What happened to "turtles all the way down"? Ah, but turtles from where? Some post-World War nation yet to be created? And where the heck is the American eagle? "You have to remember," Masha Vorontsova of World Wildlife Fund Russia tells the *Guardian* in the article previously mentioned, "that bears are natural scavengers. In the U.S. and Canada you can't leave any food in tents in national parks." Ms. Vorontsova says nothing about leaving corpses in tents. Truth is, you can't leave any food in birdfeeders. And have I mentioned Sputnik? He feels the barkest hour is just before the lawn—which may include some serious barking not only at Pokey Bottom—who perhaps from behind might remind one of the bulbous-buttocked current U.S. president, Donald J. Trump—but also at Masha Vorontsova, who tells us that Russian bears are fast learners. "In Karelia," she says, "one bear learned how to open a coffin. He then taught others." And what can we say about Yogi but "Smarter than the average bear"? I understand this aesthetic construction has possibly taken a grizzly turn, but I hear tell my niece Lauren claims she wouldn't mind being eaten by a bear after her decease. Now, Trump's pick for the Secretary of Education, the very Christian whitey-white beneficiary of the pyramid scheme that is Amway, apparently feels that Laurie is wrong, the darkest power is just above the pawns, and that grizzly bears are such a threat to the variety of for-profit, Christian education she wishes to provide down the nation's throat that she believes firearms should be standard issue in our schools. We can only hope that those seriously mentally ill persons who can find help nowhere else may find comfort in the knowledge that there will be plenty of employment available for them as soon as they pick out their handguns or rifles and ammo and vests and explosives and then look into getting their gun cards—no hurry on that last item. The cartoon Russian Bear was often pictured as clumsy and ill-mannered; then again, the American Eagle is "of bad moral character" according to none other than Benjamin Franklin. Karen goes to throw out the garbage, and that's it for Sputnik! He's out the door and down the road to chase Pokey Bear out of Louise's yard. Karen and Bill chase the little fellow down the road, their only hope being that Pokey Bottom will be true to his name and Sputnik will run rings around him. Karen's told me it's difficult up there in Barronett when almost everyone she knows has voted for Trump. (It's different for Bill, who works in a groovy co-op— organic food and liberalism galore.) Of course, Karen claims the chickens will come home to roost when the local farmers can't find any cheap, undocumented labor come harvest time. Okay, you know that *chickens* thing is a metaphor. I want to be clear because apparently some of Bernie Sanders' followers thought that when he said we need a revolution that he meant *we need a revolution*. Well, Ms. Masha Vorontsova, are you happy now? You and your smarty-pants, dig-up-the-politburo-of-the-bygone-days bears. You think your bears are so advanced? Well, let me tell you something: a bunch of Michigan bears have just kidnapped Betsy DeVos. They are refrigerating her as we speak (so to speak). The terrorist bears have yet to release their demands. Except that they'd rather there be no jokes about *grizzly remains*. A day goes by and Trump tweets his usual about Andrew Jackson winning the anvil-tossing battle at the Valley of the Forge and signs an executive order renaming the office that he holds Mr. Biggliest. Two days later Sputnik strolls into Bill and Karen's yard. He smells of skunk and is loaded with woodticks. He needs delousing, fumigating, and debriefing. But he acts like somewhere out in the woods there's a big bear with the birdseed beat out of him. He is oh, so proud, somewhat like, on occasion, God willing and the people resisting, we all may be.

Seven Deadlies: A Prose Sestina [a.k.a., The Rifle out the Sixth Floor Window Looking to Catch Your Eye]

Lazy day in Vietnam for Henry Cabot Lodge after he's not raised a finger and aided the coup that killed Nhu and Diem. Was it avarice placed the call to Sylvia Odio, told her about his crazy buddy Leon Oswald, who's liable to do anything? Imagine that one melancholy afternoon a prose poem envies the sestina. Insatiable memories of Havana bedevil the nights of Santos Trafficante and Johnny Roselli worse than RFK's investigations, haunt the unwritten lines of amateur poet and gentleman spy James Angleton more than the borrowed music of Ezra Pound or T.S. Eliot, and perturb the boozy stupors of super-spy Bill Harvey beyond all deliriums. Born under Truman, the CIA enters the world with patriotic aplomb, plausible deniability, and obscure bloodlust. Some argue it was John F. Kennedy's *hubris* caused his assassination, but those people—whether pundits, reporters or politicians—while they make the Kennedy Administration sound tragic and doomed and all—uppity public and possibly naughty private actions of the rich and powerful challenge the gods or their laws resulting in classical comeuppance and downfall—given the back-channel communications with Nikita Khrushchev to end the missile crisis or begin the test ban treaty, or with Fidel Castro to reestablish diplomatic and trade relations with Cuba—they've equated *hubris* with second-guessing Cold War consensus—and, okay, maybe some naughty privates too, à la hanky-panky at the White House pool. While the long fluorescent-lit corridor down which Allen Dulles rages . . .

Flickering fluorescent light, shadowed faces and wrath down the long corridor. Seymour Hersh claims it was Jack Kennedy's concupiscence that undermined his presidency, said claim perhaps limiting the role of the Joint Chiefs, or downplaying David Atlee Phillips, or neglecting various Cold Warriors in Congress, or brushing aside Richard Helms, or understating the performance of "Maurice Bishop," or trivializing Alpha 66 and other anti-Castro Cuban groups, or diminishing Allen Dulles, or soft-pedaling James Angleton, or downgrading Johnny Roselli, or de-emphasizing William Harvey, or disregarding Antonio Veciana, or glossing over Santos Trafficante, or negating David Atlee Phillips, or minimizing David Morales, or underrating Herminio Diaz Garcia, or making light of David Atlee Phillips, or pooh-poohing J. Edgar Hoover, or overlooking Frank Sturgis and E. Howard Hunt, or selling short an aforementioned military-industrial complex, or did I mention David Atlee Phillips? Super-spy in his own mind, Lee Harvey figures he's schmoozed these furtive Cubans, his ticket to Havana, but they're anti-Castro thugs and he's one way to Palookaville. From the Latin *rapere* "to snatch," the word *rapacious*, as in, "The rapacious business leaders and Wall Street vampires who hated Jack Kennedy seem an unlikely subject for a prose poem that would emulate the sestina." Apparently, Henry Cabot Lodge had no love or happy thoughts for John F. Kennedy, only grumbles and envy. Say good-bye, Vietnam and Cuba, to the indolent non-interventionist days of the young United States. And pretty much the same news reporters, gluttons for a grim story, who'd print anything Joe McCarthy mentioned at deadline.

Four hundred plus insatiable reporters in our nation's media with agency ties to any fairy tale emplotted by the CIA. Meanwhile, squinting around the murky movie theater, Lee Harvey Oswald all but envies his former self, stuck in a radio and television plant in Minsk. The FBI fails to investigate mobsters, right-wing corporate bosses, and maniacal *Batistianos*, but J. Edgar's boys are not at all slothful when it comes to tailing Martin Luther King, Jr., and tapping his phone. Yet the prose poem imagines conjugal relations with the sestina, or failing conjugal relations, extra-marital relations, sort of like Marilyn Monroe and "Mr. President," or if not extra-marital relations, perhaps a peep at the naked sestina, who'll whisper, again and again, sweet *teleutons* in the prose poem's ear. Talk about a proud nation wherein "a profound intra-administration division is resolved by an assassination." CIA propagandist David Atlee Phillips and his Castro-phobic colleagues, who figure most people will believe anything, want us to buy an angry Fidel smuggling commie hit men into Dallas; meanwhile, Supreme Court Chief Justice Earl Warren, one-time CIA head Allen Dulles, and Presidents Lyndon Johnson and Gerald Ford, highly respected U.S. government authorities who figure people will believe most anything, want us to swallow a Lee Harvey Oswald acting on his own out of "a deep-rooted resentment of all authority." Was it avarice sent Jack Ruby to Cuba, put him in touch with casino mobsters in prison?

Or maybe avarice disguised as patriotism ran the guns from the Midwest through Chicago to New Orleans and Miami and into the counter-revolutionary training camps for Alpha 66, the

International Anti-Communist Brigade, certain members of the Student Revolutionary Directorate, and their friends in the Central Intelligence Agency. Laissez faire days in South Vietnam as corrupt military coup topples corrupt military coup and Henry Cabot Lodge dreams of the proud moment when he was chosen as Richard Nixon's running mate. Allen Dulles remembers the days when he called the shots and the fluorescent lights flicker and buzz and he could just blow his top! Nostalgia is a type of envy of the past, thinks the prose poem, imagining this somehow relates to a newfound fondness for the sestina. From the Latin *dolere* "to suffer or give pain," prefixed by *in-*, meaning "not," we have the purpose of the Warren Commission. You wonder if the moniker "Leon" is supposed to link Oswald to Trotsky, a truly insatiable, world-hungry commie—leader of the Russian revolution, founder of the Fourth International, and opponent of the notion of socialism in one measly country. Here's Ruby oogling the girls in the strip club.

The girls are stripping down to tasseled pasties and g-strings and Ruby's assuming JFK would oogle these girls too. Alpha 66 disagrees with the Kennedy Administration regarding whether it's downright slothful to encourage the Castro regime to sever ties with the Soviet Union rather than overthrowing Fidel. As if they were real piggies outside a gone-out-of-business all-you-can-eat buffet, the casino mobsters cannot get Havana out of their minds. The prose poem imagines with pride what a coup it would be to steal the sestina's thunder. The Joint Chiefs incensed that their so-called Commander-in-Chief leaves the room in a huff when they merely mention their plans for preemptive nuclear strike on the Soviet Union. Nikita Khrushchev firmly believes that greed drives capitalism and drives its adherents entirely insane enough to start a third world war, and he can only hope that John F. Kennedy, unlike the bulk of US politicians, corporate heads, intelligence agents and military mucketty-mucks can think his way beyond news headlines like, "If Peace Comes, What Happens to Business?" The Europeans rightly envy us, Allen Dulles informs the Warren Commission, because European assassinations are foul conspiracies whereas here in America they're always simply the work of loony loners.

There's John Wilkes Booth, envying the European conspirators who are at least credited for their conspiring together to commit a political assassination. The anger, the rage, the vexation, the pique, the fury, the acrimony, the crossness, the exasperation, the distemper, the outrage, the ire, the ire, the venomousness, the annoyance, the virulence, the wrath, the bitterness, the bile, the heat under the collar, *el enojo*, the churlishness, the indignation, the ill humor, the slow burn, the irritability, the choler, the spleen, the spleen, the pissed-offedness, *la furia*, the discomposure, the ill will, the rancor, the vindictiveness, the bad blood, the spite, the dadblammittiness, the downright displeasure of the anti-Castro Cubans at President Kennedy's refusal to back their play at the Bay of Pigs. How many money-grubbing mobsters and power-coveting *Batistianos* kicked out of Cuba along with their CIA fellow travelers would it take to screw in the lightbulb of assassination? Arlen Specter wants you to know: a magic bullet is not a lazy bullet. And whom do we find boozing until 3 a.m. on November 22, 1963, but the

Secret Service agents assigned to the president's motorcade. The Latin *cupere* means "to desire," which reminds Sam Giancana of Judith Campbell Exner, Jack Ruby of the strippers, Lee Harvey Oswald of his intrigues, the anti-Castro Cubans of Anastasio Somoza or Augusto Pinochet, J. Edgar Hoover of his secret files, Lyndon Baines Johnson of the White House, the Joint Chiefs of their warheads, Seymour Hersh of his investigative reputation, Jack Kennedy of Jackie (and Mary Meyer and Judith Campbell Exner and Marilyn Monroe and Ellen Rometsch and various poolside beauties), and the prose poem of the beautiful, intricate, and—may we say it?—perhaps-an-iota-perplexing sestina. Talk about a proud organization: John F. Kennedy not yet in the ground and the CIA's engineered evidence of Oswald at the Soviet and Cuban embassies in Mexico City, in contact with the KGB's head assassin in the Western Hemisphere and collecting money from shady-looking Cubans for purposes most subversive.

Or talk about a proud organization: not twenty-four hours after the assassination and the FBI's decided Lee Harvey Oswald's a lone gunman who got off three shots on a crappy Mannlicher-Carcano in five seconds from the sixth floor of the Texas School Book Depository while eating lunch several floors below, and in line with its findings, the bureau disappears conflicting witness testimony, the presidential vehicle, Kennedy's and Governor Connally's clothing, Oswald's rifle and the paper bag it came in, as well as much of Lee Harvey's former associations, memberships, friendships, comings-and-goings, altercations, inclinations and wherewithals. From the Latin *insatiabilis*, our description of the prose poem's impetuous attraction to and mad yearning for not only the glory of the sestina but also the power of a "lone gunman" theory. Meanwhile, introduced by Frank Sinatra, John Kennedy and Judith Campbell Exner had an affair while she remained buddy-buddy with Mafia figures John Roselli and Sam Giancana; and brought together by Lyndon Johnson's pal Bobby Baker, John Kennedy and Ellen Rometsch had a fling though unbeknownst to him (shades of John Profumo), she was maybe a Soviet spy; but no greater jollies were had than those of J. Edgar, master of listening in and peeping, bugging and creeping. After the peaceful resolution of the Cuban missile crisis, the powers behind the electoral veneer go absolutely spelunkers-in-the-wrong-cavern, batshit-aspiration rabid. Such was the magic bullet's greed for human flesh that it entered President Kennedy's back and exited his throat only to enter and exit Governor Connally's back, wrist and thigh, and to be found on Connally's gurney in Parkland Hospital unmarked by blood, human tissue, or clothing, as if waiting to be fired again at the next president who failed to understand business first and war forever. Late in the night and James Jesus Angleton, acquaintance of Ezra Pound and T.S. Eliot and something of a poet in his own right, if he may say so himself, concerns himself with a complexity of slant rhymes on Possum's phrase "wilderness of mirrors"—Angleton's own objective correlative for the feeling an agent gets as he is drawn further into the world of intelligence and intrigue—something besides "churlishness of murders"—but the memories of Havana haunt him and drunken Bill Harvey outing Angleton's own mentor as KGB and *Batistianos* into whose ears he's whispered or had others whisper—something besides "we'll digress in error"—not to mention out-acted by David Atlee Phillips—that's "Mr. Bishop" to you, buddy—who could so utterly dissemble—that's "Dallasemble" to you, pal—not that the CIA was demonstrably, unambiguously involved, nor that he envies for a moment the leisurely and lucrative careers of certain widely acclaimed Modern poets, not at all, nor their abilities—at all. Lazy day in Dallas as the presidential vehicle slows to a stop at Dealey Plaza to make the turn.

After sloth and greed, business as usual: Richard M. Nixon steps out of Air Force One and hoists his arms up into the air. After envy, gluttony, and lust, what can a prose poem tell you (even one that, perhaps sinning, adds a *teleuton*, outdoes the sestina) but that assassination makes an ass of the shooter and a bigger ass of the nation. After pride and wrath, business as usual on the way to despair: cities burn, wages freeze, bombs burst in Southeast Asian skies, gas prices rise, and industrial jobs disappear.

Is This a Bad Time?

Rahm's visiting his old buddy Bruce's Montana ranch—bourbon and Big Sky Country. Maybe a chuckle or two over their last little Twitter spat about that crazy Father Pfleger shutting down the goddamn Dan Ryan with his march against violence. "More bourbon, buddy?" "Maybe just one more swallow. Fly fishing tomorrow." When who should barge in but the Hammonds, son and father, Steven and Dwight, newly pardoned by their president, throwing a bit of meat to his base. Son and father, backslapping and hooting, open carrying AR-15s, acorn and tree—but, no, they've all been pretty well burned down. Bruce looks inconvenienced and pissed, "This is my property!" And Rahm: "Do you know who I am?!" And the patriot movement of Oregon so happy these gentlemen will be coming home right after they let Bruce and Rahm know how they helped out: "No need for fly fishing. We done massacred those trout. Woowee! You can do a lotta damage with a bump stock on your AR-15!" "Yep, just reach down and getchu some. They're lying right there on the surface of the water." But at the White House no one's happy. Reports are in: the Confederate statues are marching away, pedestalled equestrians or pedestrians, from every city and state, marching away. "To where?" cries Trump, blows his nose, toots his own horn, bosses everyone around, "Get the FBI right on it! And the NSA! And ICE!" Not too far from the permineralization going south past the Mississippi Petrified Forest along the Natchez Trace, and—as Beverly and I have found—before you know it, we've reached the Stoneyhome

Plantation House and Used-to-be Slave Labor Camp: "Here at Stoneyhome, when young master required a shower, he'd arrange his butt-naked self in this here clawfoot tub, and one of the most trusted of slaves who had the honor would climb the step ladder at the rear of the tub and from a bucket ever-so-gently pour water down upon his youthful nubile pink Caucasian form." Back in the US, back in the US, back in the USA plenty of swastika shtuppers and white-hooded white supremacists still go for this sort of thing, what with Klokards and Kludds, with Kleagles and Klaliffs, and—*Mein Kampf!*—how wonderfully Trump speaks their language: "You can do anything you want . . . Grab 'em by the pussy!" But the first things grabbed are indigenous peoples' land rights, water rights, burial grounds, fisheries, and wetlands. Eight pipeline projects up and running natural gas liquids, crude oil, and fracked natural gas. Also grabbed, nearly 200 Inauguration Day demonstrators, each looking at sixty years in the slammer. Soon state legislators introduce bills to protect motorists who run over demonstrators: Rhode Island, North Dakota, North Carolina, Tennessee, and, of course, Texas. And, of course, Florida. In *The Turner Diaries*—a fictional representation of the race war stored in Trump's brain, updated from *The Birth of a Nation*, Woodrow Wilson's electroshock therapy ("like writing history with lightning! Yee-haw!"), conveniently screened in the White House—the white people's homeland winds up in southern California, includes the Sierra Madre and the Mojave, a fictional people's just deserts. Or there's the "Carolina Free State," a 1980s ideal held by certain murderous southern Klans, in which North and South Carolina would provide the white ethnos with their white ethno-state. The search for white Elmo? The search for a place for the Trump-sponsored 311-foot-tall bronze statue of Christopher Columbus? The search for whiter whites? Damn you, DNA!! The Christian Patriot Defense League proposes the "Mid-America Survival Area," from the east end of Colorado to the west end of West Virginia. All these competing wannabe white ethno-states would, of course, entail the voluntary ingress of white people and the voluntary-or-else egress of nonwhite people. When we ask the docent at Stoneyhome if we may see the old slave quarters, her complexion becomes a more complex shade of pink as she replies, "Oh, those! They're not here anymore." You've got to wonder if they've also marched away, or if the Confederate statues have come for them. Or maybe they've been hauled away by the humungous Columbus, designed and welded by Russian artist, Zurab Tsereteli, and composed of, Trump once claimed, "$40 million dollars' worth of bronze"—and that's at pre-tariff prices. My comrade and darling wife, Beverly is off to the National Education Association (NEA) convention in Minneapolis right after the illegitimate Supreme Court's latest illegitimate majority ruling in *Janus vs. American Federation of State, County, and Municipal Employees* restrains and hoods precedent, waterboards logical argument, and allows right-to-work cant to weaponize the First Amendment, so that the money wielded by corporations, banks, and hedge funds equals free speech—thanks to *Citizens United vs Democratic Elections*—but the union's money, even for bargaining, let alone for political spending, isn't free speech at all because, uh, because . . . oh, right! it's the dues of members who deserve their own free speech, which, in this case would mean refusing to pay dues to their unions, said unions being the only way working people can defend themselves from neoliberal depredations, which reminds us of another time a few years back when Rahm and Bruce were at Rauner's Wyoming ranch high-fiving each other after closing down fifty public schools and preventing the Chicago Teachers' Union strike and the strike-supporting parents and students from thwarting their plans. Rahm says, "When you said those parents 'don't understand what's going on inside their schools,' it made me feel like back after Barack Obama was first elected and I told all his supporters who believed in change to SHUT THE FUCK UP! You should've seen the constipated looks on those MoveOn people's faces!" Rauner returns the compliment, "You looked so manly when you said that 'we have parents that don't know how to be parents!' Whatta guy!" and he slaps Rahm on the back. "Ouch!" Well, skip forward a few years to yesterday and red state teachers start striking: West Virginia, Oklahoma, Arizona, Colorado, North Carolina . . . This is when I realize that with the great power of prose poetry, I have great responsibility. So I go undercover, find out that in neo-Nazi circles and under the picture of Andrew Jackson in the White House, "88" means "Heil Hitler!" and "The Fourteen Words" are "We must secure the existence of our people and a future for white children," which tells me that the white nationalists and white supremacists and militias and patriots and Christian Identity racists and their evangelical pals haven't figured out yet that there's no such thing as white people, so I'm off, trying to pick up the trail of the Confederate pedestalled equestrian or pedestrian statues, maybe head 'em off at the pass. This is right about the time that Rebekah Mercer and her silent-partner father begin their search for the biophysiochemist/

alchemist who might could devise a de-permineralization process via which the Confederate statues could be transmogrified back around to the real Robert E. Lee, Jefferson Davis, and their creepy racist rapist pals. No wonder Donald Trump's so angry at Angela Merkel: no statues of Hitler. He's angry too at London's Sadiq Khan for allowing the Big Baby Trump balloon to fly over Parliament and Big Ben, making him feel unwelcome. And he's on the phone to General Mattis: "The Confederate statues are marching away! The horsey ones too! You got to find them or who knows where it will end? Jefferson? Jackson? Will I walk away before I'm even commemmorororted?" David Duke thought pretty much like those Mid-America-type Christian Patriots except he mapped out a "New Africa" for Black people in the South, a Jewish "New Israel" on the east coast, "Alta California" for Latinx people in the Southwest—he wanted to give them the Sierra Madre and the Mojave—and the rest would be the "White Bastion"—*bastion* here in its sense of "stronghold," as in, as my dictionary tells me, "the last *bastion* of male privilege." Speaking of male privilege, the Senate Judiciary Committee pretty well understands that rape is about power. Why, rape or attempted rape or at least sexual harassment has lately become an unwritten qualification for Supreme Court openings. The colossal Columbus, titled *The Birth of the New World*, offered to Miami, Fort Lauderdale, Cleveland, Baltimore, Columbus, Ohio (of course), and New York City, and described by citizens and critics as "Chris Kong," "an exotically banal hundred-and-fifty-story phallus," "graceless as a herd of brontosaurus . . . . configured in the shape of an exploded hydrant," and "From Russia with Ugh," never did find a home in the continental US but, by some evil twist of fate and colonialism, comes to grace Arecibo, Puerto Rico. Speaking of which, Trump is angry too at Carmen Yulin Cruz, the mayor of San Juan, for Hurricane Maria, for living on an island surrounded by water, and for holding him responsible for the 2,975 deaths due to government neglect. Oh, wait, here's an email from Illinois Governor Bruce Rauner: "Click here to leave your union." But we have to give Ronald Reagan his due—by kicking off his 1980 presidential campaign in Neshoba County, Mississippi, where three civil rights workers (James Chaney, Andrew Goodman, and Michael Schwerner) were kidnapped, murdered, and disappeared for forty-four days in 1964, he emboldened the white supremacist movement, and then he set the tone for the far right by spreading the neoliberal dictum, "government is not the solution to our problem; government is the problem." Within a few years the white supremacists are calling the federal government a Zionist Occupation Government—"ZOG" for short—militarizing themselves, and plotting their white ethno-state, that, given their druthers, will one day cover the whole territory of the present northwest United States, what is currently Oregon, Washington, Idaho, Wyoming, and Montana. Wow! Looks like Bruce will be able to keep both his ranches! But not so fast. The Hammond boys, father and son, Dwight and Steven, crazy-as-loons, batshit-on-the-loose white folks, finally pick up the clue phone and realize Rahm and Bruce are far from appreciative, so they leave in a huff, complain on the internet—not the dark web (obviously), but deeper down, way the hell down to the whitey-white web, where whitest supremacists of the US, NATO nations, Israel, and Russia keep in touch and propagandize, call rallies, trade ideas, provoke lone wolves, and spin off underground cells of three or more bigots who can terrorize without fear of the above-ground bigshot bigots getting busted. So, who drops by the Montana ranch but a cell of three murderous white supremacists on vacation from separating members of immigrant families as agents of ICE. We'll call them Rock, Hard Place, and Chad. They tie the politicians to kitchen chairs, and they're spilling gasoline and kerosene and acetone and benzene all over the ranch house. "You betcha this place'll burn right down," chuckles Hard Place. "Yep," Rock agrees, "And then we're going to Wyoming to burn down your other ranch house. We're taking your fishing gear too." And Chad asks, "You guys got a coupla, three beers? This here's thirsty work!" Rock pulls from an inside pocket of his orange vest (deer hunting, you know) his 1950s vintage Zippo lighter engraved with the Gadsden flag (rattlesnake curling upward from the logo: "Don't Tread on Me!"—with the exclamation point for emphasis). Despite her cash inducements, Rebekah Mercer's scientists can't deal with the whole de-permineralization postulation since it's based on impermanent things they have been trained by the far right to doubt: climate change, evolutionary change, changing minds, changing mores, changing prospects for the future, changing immoral laws, changing underwear—*Ubi, O ubi, sunt meum sub ubi?* Rebekah, dejected, groans and gripes, "Not all the bronze in the BrontoColumbus can help The Donald with those tiny, tiny hands!" You'd think the evangelicals would be upset, being passed over as far as the great white ethno-state's concerned, but they smile knowingly, then run off giggling and praying: "Jesus O Jesus PenceyPence/ God's will O

Jesus PrezzyPence/ no cake for homosexuills/ Jesus Jesus O God'swill/ PrezzyPencey O Rapture! PrezzyPence!" Elsewhere, a nearby far-right-wing Christian Identity-type militia member, most likely an Oath Keeper, and one who was at the occupation of the Malheur National Wildlife Refuge, stops by Rauner's ranch to see if the Hammond fellas want to go hunting for maybe some white-tailed deer—out of season—and mountain goat, grizzly bear, elk and kangaroo rat; Canadian lynx, caribou, American bison, cougar, and moose; red fox, jumping mice, porcupine, muskrats, bobcats, mule deer, and raccoon; and he manages to save Bruce and Rahm before he realizes what he's doing. He does pick up a pretty nifty zippo lighter though—scorched, but with the snake still as severed as ever. Speaking of Rauner, while Rahm calls for an Uber, Bruce blasts another email: "Free speech. Rah, rah. Click here to leave your union!" How do we block these things? All the while, the white supremacists and KKKhristians wonder, "Where's white Waldo? Where's white nationalist GI Joe?" Soon the cry goes up among crazy white people, "We want a Merry Christmas and a white Jesus too!" But we have to give the Koch brothers, Charles and David—libertarians in government, fascists in business, Big Oil and bigger assholes—their due: "from the withdrawal from the Paris Climate Accord to the massive tax cut for corporations and the one-percenters to the gutting of federal regulations and turning the EPA into a clownlike organization." Oh, but we have to give Betsy DeVos credit too: computer traffic from the Russian Alfa Bank not only to Trump Tower but also to Spectrum Health of Michigan, owned by the DeVos family, puts Betsy DeVos—vulture capital's favorite Secretary of Education, and college rapists' too—right in the middle of the dizzying scandal of Russia's proceeding by the negation of the negation always already interfered with the 2016 election, otherwise democratic but for gerrymandering, electoral college chicanery, superPACs, purged voter rolls, closed polling places in nonwhite neighborhoods, media interference, and felony disqualification laws, so that the Exploited and Oppressed People's Chorus (aka the Chorus) takes the stage in the field of browned and brittle grasses where the slave quarters once stood on the Stoneyhome property, and they sing: "Has the Kochtopus inadvertently cleared the way/ for Putin, or are the Russian oligarchs serving as distracting/ window dressing for the Kochian defenestration of/ the last vestiges of US democracy? And how is it that/ either way white supremacists fit right in?" Betsy DeVos orders her Office for Civil Rights confirm her notion that programs supporting women at Yale and the University of Southern California are discriminating. . .against men. Forgive and forget? Exactly that! DeVos is forgetting about the program whereby indentured ex-students have their loans forgiven. Meanwhile, unknown to all except the people of Arecibo, Puerto Rico—and they are, frankly, quite relieved—*The Dawn of the New World* shambles into the sea, slogs along the bottom, lumbers its way to Orlando, Florida, and right outside a certain branded, super-exploitive, ratfink amusement park meets the Confederate statues, equestrian and otherwise, melds with them, and with Joe Arpaio— of the mis-spending, misconduct, abuse, torture, wrongful arrests and murder-type law enforcement, recently pardoned by his president, more meat for the beast—de-permineralizes with them into one skunky-breathed, foul-mouthed, Cyclopean

Columbosuarus, name of MAGAMORE (*Magamurus racistis fascisticuffs*). Oh, for Chrissakes! Another text from Rauner: "Use your First Amendment right to leave your union!" And can you believe Joe Arpaio? With the gargantuan Columbus and all those Confederate statues, the Columbosaurus was not racist enough? But we have to give the Clintons their due: where would we be without their call to freakout about crack babies and Black super-predators, and police police police the neighborhoods and overfill the prisons until Black and Latinx citizens can speak Gulag, to transmogrify welfare to workfare or fare thee well, to NAFTA-nuke Mexican agricultural and US industrial employment, to deregulate the financial sector for an Enron around mortgage hedge fund world banking crash, all while white–male–presidential–privilege Bill gets a little something on the side. Still undercover, I learn that these crazy racist Christian Identity people believe the Old and New Testaments were written for and about the Aryan race, and that mistranslations and an evil (of course) Jewish (ditto) conspiracy have led the world to believe otherwise. "We wish you a Merry Christmas! And a white Jesus too!" Meanwhile, Beverly and the Higher Ed. Caucus and others in the NEA join in with the Families Belong Together march in Minneapolis. Teachers' demands everywhere not being met, the red state strikes resume, this time also including Kansas, Indiana, Wisconsin, Idaho, Montana, and Nebraska. "That's half the ethno-state!" cry certain murderous, god-fearing, ZOG-hating white-supremacists. A sinkhole develops on the White House lawn, and shortly thereafter a bolt of lightning hits the White House, knocking Andrew Jackson's painting off the wall. Meanwhile, the search for said white ethno-state is slowed by the disturbing knowledge (found in this prose poem and elsewhere) that once upon a USA, only those of British, Germanic, or Nordic ancestry were considered to be "white." Neo-Nazi to Klansman cries, "White, the fuck?!! What about the Italians, Greeks, Irish, Spaniards, Lithuanians, Ukrainians, Russians, and Catholic Arabs?" When those ethnicities applied for whiteness, Uncle Sam replied, "Get in line! One at a time! And get ready to convincingly demonstrate the proper racism." The oath-keeping crowd gets distracted by these facts, loses its way, and burns down Stoneyhome by mistake. Then, considering their responsibility for the fire, said patriots run through the briars and they run through the brambles and they run many places where the rabbit wouldn't go! With a "good riddance" to the guilt-ridden, fleet-footed patriots, the left plans to launch Baby Trump balloons over every US city, town, and rural community so that a certain orange person is unwelcome from sea to shining sea. But how to discombobulate, un-de-permineralize and dismantle the Columbosaurus? Meanwhile, Mike Pence and his evangelical minions root through frat houses looking for serial rapists to man—and they do mean *man*—the nation's highest court. Magamore tromps its way to the Federal Triangle in D.C. and blasts EPA headquarters—PHOOOSH!— with its awful breath! The EPA headquarters empties and shrivels. In response the Chorus sings: "Magamore, you think you're so powerful, but/ you should think again because Scott Pruitt has/ already been there and done that!" Evangelist to evangelist says, "I thought Armageddon was supposed to happen in Israel, on the hill of Megiddo." The latter replies, "Plague of mosquitoes?" Sunoco's fracked-gas pipeline in Pennsylvania blows; from Pittsburgh to

Philadelphia, nobody lights a match; everybody holds their breath. K-12 teachers are now out on strike in every red state—and blue state teachers are out in solidarity with their red state comrades!—even as the White House press corps are gathering for Sarah Huckabee Sanders' statement denying the disappearance of the disappeared Confederate statues and introducing the president's proposal for an all-male, all-elite schooled, all-Christian, all-sex-offender, super-best Supreme Court. What a body!—makes a certain kind of president want to grab them by their gavels with his tiny presidential hands—to overturn Roe v. Wade. Giggles and "PrezzyPence"'s are heard—the evangelicals trust in Jesus as their Pence dispenser. Meanwhile, outside the NEA Convention, here come the militarized police—pepper ball guns, ballistic shields, AR-15s and Glocks, stun grenades, tasers, flash bang grenades, and shotguns—Remington and Benelli—Colt handguns, body armor, eyewear, and Scott Pruitt-approved weatherproof tactical pants (he wore in his $43,000 soundproof phone booths). Also, a tank and an ARV. And Jeff Sessions with a bullhorn, "Surrender now, you Higher Ed. terrorists!" Elsewhere, the Dakota Access pipeline leaks humungous oil spills all through Iowa and southern Illinois, and a certain Uber slides into a multitudinous oil pool tenebrous. Magamore stomps over to the Robert F. Kennedy Department of Justice Building—"Oh, jeepers!" say the Hammonds, father and son, Dwight and the other, who all they wanted was to illegally hunt deer and cover their tracks by burning down forests, "This is out of control!"—and—PHOO-OOSH!—empties and shrivels the DOJ. The Chorus responds: "Give it up, Magamore, for Jeff Sessions and the Trump Klan/ have already whitified and corrupted

Justice, and/ you are nothing but a metaphor besides." Grizzly bears eat Betsy DeVos. The Plantation Pipe Line (yes, Kinder Morgan actually calls it that) bursts, and gasoline, jet fuel, and diesel fuel besplooshes Pennsylvania Avenue from Capitol to White House. "Meta-Huh?" grunts Magamore and dissipates. But only momentarily. Not unlike systemic racism, it finds new form—as toxic demonic hegemonic fog. While a whole passel of dominionist Christian Identity patriots, carrying their own gasoline and kerosene and acetone and benzene, head for the Malheur National Forest, still-hungry grizzly bears eat Steven Miller. Cougars eat Jeff Sessions. The Giant Baby Trump balloons go up all over the USA. Wolverines, raccoons, and weasels eat Mike Pence and his Supreme Court nominees. Evangelist helpers flee, shouting, "Thoughts and prayers! Thoughts and prayers!!" A Bruce Rauner email, requesting assistance (union or non-union) escaping a certain tenebrous pool, goes right to everyone's spam folder. The discombobulated runaway patriots stop off at the White House to get their bearings and enjoy a cigar. VOOOOSH! "Don't look now," says Hard Place, "but I think another slave-built fancy mansion just got burned down or blowed up, one." "Been there/ Done that," the Chorus sings, but Chad's asking, "Did anybody bring along some beer? This here's pretty thirsty work." "I like beer," interjects Brett Kavanaugh. "That wasn't the question," Chad retorts, "Can't you give a straight answer to one damn question?" But here comes Trump's base: self-proclaimed patriots, KKKhristians and Christian Identity warriors for the Aryan Christ, neo-Nazis, Ku Klux Klanners, anti-Semites and Islamophobes, plain old home-grown white supremacists and sexists, perverts and sadists (elected and unelected, religious and secular), psychopathic incels, Russian operatives and a few oligarchs, Saudi and Israeli lobbyists, grass-roots Tea Party-type GOPers, huge numbers of patriotic militia, border patrol, and ICE agents, significant numbers of AFT, FBI, CIA, NSA agents, and a great number of Fox News-, whitey-white web-, and Trump-administration-policy-driven lone wolves. Oh, and a handful of kooks in home-made Space Force attire. Everyone is heavily armed—AR-15s with bump stocks, mostly. And just before the toxic fog descends, somebody—The Higher Ed. Caucus of the NEA? The red and blue state strikers? The human race?—pulls the metaphorical emergency break.

"Stone Free"?

Spinoza claims that, given consciousness, the stone thrown in any given direction thinks that it's going where it wants. This is pretty much, you know, a given, and the same with the chair that Allan leans back in until it falls over in the group therapy session for the entertainment of the drunk drivers, wife beaters, drug abusers, and the rest of the court-ordered captive audience with whom he's stuck. The therapist laughs her head off too. Me, I've noticed the way the dogs' water bowl positions itself perfectly so that I'll step on its side and flip water all over foot and hardwood floor. The champagne flutes that happen to stand perilously close to the edge of the counter. The kitchen cabinet door wide open and waiting for your noggin. It makes one think: perhaps consciousness flows through all things in greater or lesser degrees, and perhaps the lesser degrees are *morally* lesser but, in some sense, more devious, more subtle—plotting to take over the world one mishap at a time. The unscooped dog poop brimming to the inevitable shoetop with potential, ambition, and a vile sense of delight.

*

Marx may have thought himself some kinda materialist, but he had his quirks and foibles. Phrenology, for criminy's sake. The very stones cry out. Not in a sympathetic kinda way: "He wants to read the bumps on his noggin, we'll give him some bumps on the old noggin."

*

Plash. Plash. Plashedy-plash. Yes, it's a lovely day. Seventy-two degrees and mostly sunny except for that occasional cloud tumbling by above. Oh, and look at the birds up there calling to one another. Hawks do you think? Falcons? Plashedy-plash, go the horse hooves about the stream, and here we are carrying a jar to Tennessee, thinking maybe to take dominion everywhere. What was that about falcons? Widening gyres? Wild swans? Something besides the white chickens? Well, they certainly aren't moor hens calling to moor cocks. How do you know for sure at this distance? Plash, plashedy. Sounds like we might be leaving the horses behind. Just us and nature. Everything moving and wheeling and gyring in its glory. Do you think that cloud up there looks like a big rock? What do you think of that fundamentalist Christian idea that God's given human beings—or *man* rather—dominion over all? Here we are. We just go up this hill, place our tall gray jar and–*voila!*—no more slovenly wilderness. That cloud's still right over our heads. Did I mention anything about the stone being in the midst of all? Plash. THUD! Wait! Did you hear something? I think it came from back where we left those horses. By the way, where did those birds go off to? Maybe this is a good enough spot. Let's put down the jar and get the hell out of here. WHACK! SMASH! So much for the jar. Run! Run! WHACKO! Oh, he's felled! My kingdom for a horse! Wait a minute! Is this some kind of devilish devious joke? The wilderness seems to be rising up around his poor stone-bonkered noggin. ZIP! ZING! Ohmygosh! Ohsweetdominion! No time for aesthetics! These stones have a mind of their—BONK!

"A Tree, a Rock, a Cloud": I can't tell you how much stones love that story. They think it packs a wallop! They believe it will lead us to worship them.

*

The clock radio goes off and you jump out of bed with relief: "Phewie! It was all just a dream." Bob Dylan's singing about how everybody must get stoned. Off to the shower. Turn on the water and— No water? But I paid the water bill. Step in to take a better look and SCALDING HOT WATER FOR CRIMINY'S SAKE! Jump from the tub and stub your toe on the radiator. Hobble out of the bathroom and bang your shoulder on the bedroom door frame, spin around once and fall over on the—no, next to the bed. On the floor, having knocked over the bedside table with last night's three-quarter's full water glass, now in a million pieces. And the cat's trying to lick up the water. You shoo her and swipe your hand into glass on the hardwood floor. You can see the blood, running down the side of your hand and dripping into the broken-glass water spill. The cat wants to lick that bloody danger right up. The clock radio keeps going even though it's upside down on the floor. So very near the creeping water. The cat steps into the glass-sharded puddle in search of human blood. And Joe Cocker's now singing "Let's Go Get Stoned."

*

Contrary to common belief, "the oldest profession" is being an atom. And here's something Lucretius knew: they fall straight down like stones. Now, this is before anything else, so where do the dang atoms fall *from*? No matter, because before you know it there's . . . Wait. I didn't mean there was no matter. There were those atoms falling like little stones, and next what happens . . . *Little stones* is metaphorical language. Really, we're talking about atoms falling from the heavens. And then . . . C'mon, I don't really need to stop and explain about *the heavens*, do I? *The oldest profession*? I'm trying to get to what Lucretius says about the *clin*. . .

*

And the stone thinks, If I were Spinoza, I'd believe that if I happened to throw a stone, it was no more because of my own free will than it would be of the stone's. All being one in God or Nature, it would be as if there were rocks in my head.

*

Then the story of the young Carl Jung seating himself on a stone, trying to decide who was who, and not being able to tell the difference. "No man is an island," says John Donne. But Paul Simon contradicts him, "I am a rock; I am an island." Edwin Corey goes home and puts a bullet through his head. Did he know the dark secret? Eons of the stones' congress with human flesh? Even Howard Phillips Lovecraft dared not think that his insane gibbering ancient gods could be so dastardly. And all those who tried to warn us are gone—Spinoza, Yeats, Jimi Hendrix (with the hidden messages in "Stone Free"), Laura Nyro ("Stoned Soul Picnic" with the code word "Surry," which clearly abbreviated "Let's hurry!" as in "Let's get outta here!" And "This ain't gonna be no picnic!"). I don't know, the clay people Flash Gordon could negotiate with—they had a common enemy in the Emperor Ming. And the pod people were at least authentic looking copies. And vegetable. Would stones even care about "authenticity"? Or care to keep up appearances? Before long Carl Jung is a Nazi sympathizer. So is Ezra Pound. Wyndham Lewis. T.S. Eliot. And Vivienne's in National Front getup. William Butler Yeats himself. You're thinking that was yesterday, but haven't you noticed, whomever we elect, we're ruled by Wall Street. Wall—as in "another brick in"—Street. Stone upon stone. Feels like we're trapped in a cave. Stalactites and darkness. Bat aspiration and stalagmites. I can hear the stones breathing. Moving. They're sidling up to me. And somewhere the incessant drip of dark water on cold stone.

Amazing Scientific Breakthrough:
Poem = Orgone Accumulator!

Ever pissing and moaning about his supposed predicament, sitting in St. Elizabeth's, guest of the state, free to roam the grounds, to import gourmet food and groupies, to indoctrinate and proselytize right-wing bohemian-wannabes, to gossip with his old poesy cronies, Ezra Pound complains of his room, "Stuffy as a Zeus-forsaken orgone box in here. I can't feel the creative jets of my own virility." But anyone who knows anything about orgone knows this grievance to be one good reason why the poet never received a visit from Dr. Wilhelm Reich. Now Pound's in the garden and Zeus has taken wing. Feathers fall around the cantankerous old fellow like the many wishes that his *Cantos* weren't so pedantic and boring. Even John Adams wants out of them. And I can't tell you how many Chinese dynasties. Mussolini, shot and hung upside down, feels even more put upon about being in *The Cantos*. When the birds fly South for winter, making their epic *V*s in the sky, Elizabeth Bishop will arrive from between villanelle and sestina to craft her aesthetical vision of his complexity: "This Ezra translates Confucius/ This Ezra gobbles his truffles/ This Ezra wobbles his pivot/ This Ezra propagandizes for the White Citizens Council/ And this Ezra scents his body with olibanum and oranges, nutmeg and cloves and makes love to some occult-minded cuckoo." Meanwhile Neo-Platonic philosophy is thinking there's a better world outside *The Cantos*. And the swans cohere into the blue.

*

If Wilhelm Reich were still with us, this poem would be an orgone accumulator. In many ways, Wilhelm Reich is still with us: A student admires my haircut, and, astonished, I tell the class that Beverly says it's a David Byrne cut. "Who's David Byrne?" the students ask. This reminds me that back in the late-'80s a joke went around that the undergrads didn't know Paul McCartney was in a band before Wings. These days the undergrads are after the last laugh: "My psychedelic professor probably still sings along with *Sgt. Pepper*." Well, who wants to lip-synch? In my life my haircuts have provoked comparisons to Mick Jagger, John Lennon, and Paul McCartney. Like hell, I thought three different times, waiting for a more David Byrne-like opportunity to arrive. "In My Life" is the title of a Beatles song. Though John Lennon crafted most of the song, the tune was McCartney's idea of a nod to Motown's Smokey Robinson and not David Byrne, whose big-suited opportunity hadn't yet arrived. When Paul McCartney appeared barefoot on the cover of *Abbey Road*, there sprung up a rumor he had died. "It could've been worse," Igor would say in the film *Young Frankenstein*. "It could've been raining." "Rain" is the title of another Beatles song. Imagine that album cover featuring pouring rain and the Beatles crossing and cursing Abbey Road, Paul barefoot, and in his mind the three melodic bass players of the day: himself, the Beach Boy's Brian Wilson, and Motown's James Jamerson. Like three peas in a pod or three corbies or three parts of a syllogism. And you wonder whether Mr. McCartney has ever enjoyed a friendly syllogism. This transmogrifies the poem into an orgone accumulator. "This transmogrifies the poem into an orgone accumulator," is not the title of a Beatles song.

*

Granted a metapoetical moment, we might investigate the problems of introducing to the world the concept of the poem as orgone accumulator. First, there's the general lack of acquaintance with the psychoanalytic or psychobiological, or, most importantly, psychocosmobiological theories of Dr. Reich. If the person on the street or at the poetry reading has heard of Wilhelm Reich at all, it's usually as the purveyor of nostrums that ended up on the wrong side of FDA investigations. Select individuals may know of Reich's sex-political work in Weimar Germany, the good doctor's contribution to the anti-fascist movement—and a decidedly underappreciated contribution at that. In either case, many in the audience will wonder what this quack or commie pervert has to do with concerns poetical. Secondly, since information on orgonomy is likely to be ill-informed and highly critical, persons in the audience of any aquaintance with bion experiments or the discovery of orgone may be actively hostile to the notion of a poem as an orgone accumulator, perhaps arguing, "Negative capability is about a billion miles from negatively entropic orgone energy units," or "Sitting in your orgone box, you could miss a whole season of mists and mellow fruitfulness." Those who haven't heard of the discovery of orgone may become dismayed by the ensuing debate, conceiving it to involve questions of prosody the presently uninitiated will never appreciate, much like experiments in English with quantitative verse. Even explaining the orgone accumulator itself can be a problem. For, thirdly, the days are long gone when, in order to smooth over certain difficulties elucidating the orgonomic principles involved in the accumulator, one could call up a helpful if inexact picture in the mind of an audience by way of reference to a phone booth. Yet where do we find an actual phone booth these days? The last one I recall right offhand appeared in the 1988 remake of *The Blob*, but considering the ghoulish goings-on perpetrated upon and within that particular unfortunate phone booth, it may be prudent to refrain from mentioning it. Certainly, noir films are filled with phone booths, but I'd be willing to bet you'd pick up some pretty suspicious or disconcerting or alienating or otherwise anxiety-producing connotations along with the admittedly imperfect mental picture you'd have the audience draw. Of course, there are "silver age" *Superman* comics, wherein phone booths are found in nearly every issue, but your audience might misconstrue your reference as suggesting they should disrobe in order to produce a sestina or that crafting in hendecasyllabics grants a poet x-ray vision. Next, there's orgone energy's problematic comparisons to Mesmer's "animal magnetism," Carl Reichenbach's "Odic force," and Henri Bergson's élan vital, each hypothetical bioenergy having been to some degree previously discredited as poetry's metric, stanzaic, prosodic, rhetorical, figurative, logical, surreal, tropic, syllogistic, or common sense creative substratum, though this problem may be readily resolved by pointing out that these bioenergetic analogues are mightily misnominated when contrasted with *orgone*'s proximity to so poetic a term as *orgasm*.

*

The character in the comic book worries that he might be a character in a comic book. The woman in the orgone accumulator wonders that she's a woman in an orgone accumulator. The analogous situation worries that it might not be an analogous situation. Sometimes I can almost see the thought balloon beside my head. I'm near crestfallen until I realize that it's not so much the challenges by which we are confronted in this life, but the fortitude and pizzazz with which we greet those challenges. The thought in the neo-Buddhist framework wonders if it might be a thought in a neo-Buddhist framework. The woman here in the orgone accumulator is storing up quite a bit of fortitude and pizzazz. And anyone we meet might turn out to be, you know, the Blue Beetle or Daredevil or Green Lantern or Batman or Yogi Bear or Boo Boo. The world of illusion doesn't have a worry in the world. The idea that the poem could go on like this *ad infinitum* worries that it might be held entirely within the thought balloon I can almost see beside my head.

*

When Wilhelm Reich developed his orgone accumulator, why, the news traveled from neighbor to neighbor. Right along the phone lines and maybe on the telegraph, too. The Depression was over, World War II had been favorably concluded, and nothing was going to stop us from having our own backyard bomb shelters, hula-hoops and double martinis. What's all this commotion about character armor? By the way, will we see you at the book burning tonight? Well, I don't know for sure; what's cookin'? Oh, horror comics, crime comics, Superman, Batman, Oppenheimer's security clearance, Kinsey studies, Beat poetry, Dr. Reich's books. That nice Dr. Reich? Well, not him personally. He is a white man and not a Jew, far as I know. But they will put him in prison. He did try to cure cancer, you know. Claimed it'd be as simple as sitting in this here orgone accumulator constructed of alternating layers of organic and inorganic materials. There's many an owner of tobacco fields, steel mills, copper smelters, chemical factories, and plastics plants don't want anybody snooping around cancer. Nor the government neither. Not to mention the American Medical Association. More doctors recommend Camels than any other cigarette. And just wait until that fast food industry takes off. But how do we recognize a red fascist? Oh, don't worry. They come in all colors: red, white and blue. This is what the *Pax Americana* is all about: Learning that totalitarianism doesn't have to start off as a social movement; it can get going as an economic paradigm. I don't know; I think I'd feel safer if I had my secret decoder ring.

*

Well, it's another day at the orgone accumulator repair shop of the heart. A lot of foul rags and bones lying around in the aftermath of all the necessary accumulator mending. This one's been too close to the television; that one's had a microwave oven sitting in it and been left in a damp basement besides. Sometimes I think of those Wright Brothers peering out to the horizon, wishing, "Would that people were able to transcontinentally fly like capital." H. G. Wells peering into the future and wishing, "Would that we were able to travel time as does capital." You get to thinking that capital's all powerful: a vampire or a virus or the Anti-God of John Carpenter's *Prince of Darkness*, in which perturbed priest Donald Pleasance tells us, "He lives in the smallest parts of it. Atoms. Smaller. Invisible," and you realize that the workday can be subdivided down to the nanosecond and still within each nanosecond is the portion in which the laborer works for herself and the portion in which her labor feeds the domination of Anti-God. Like we're up against some type of infernal international Godzilla, product of the postindustrial era, and probably filled with myriad T-bacilli (*T* for *Tod*, meaning *death*), formed from protein degeneration, and, let's face it, plenty dangerous. But there's one thing that people have, gosh darn it, that capital doesn't have and that's orgone energy. Reminds me we were watching *Reds* on the TV the other night and I'm wondering why's Warren Beatty using Woody Allen-type opening credits. Then I realize that John Reed's romancing Annie Hall. It's that same orgone energy pulses through us all!—the blue force that through the larva, pupa and imago stages drives the mighty, blue-eyed Lepidoptera drives the living blue matter of humanity!—and the galaxies as well! Not to mention gravity! So take heart! The tiny twin Shobijin call upon Mothra as we hasten to our orgone accumulators—tidily upkept and clean as a whistle—hoping to hustle our fearsome enemy back into the blue, blue sea. And though I've seen about thirteen hundred different ways of cooking an orgone accumulator—I've even heard that Dr. Wilhelm Reich himself was caught stinking up one of his prototypes with cigar smoke—when Steve Earle puts out that album of Townes Van Zandt tunes or when the Grateful Dead covers Dylan or the Rascals, then Mothra's got that death-dealing monster by the tail—character armor or no character armor—and she tosses and flips him like nothing to fear.

*

Beginning with a first line making mention of an organic material—formaldehyde-free particle board for instance—you can build an accumulator of your own. Next you'll need two or three alternating layers of wool batting and steel wool, but you can probably handle this in one sentence, even if it has to be constructed of more than one clause. Then you need a sentence that mentions the galvanized steel sheet that will form the interior of your accumulator. Repeat lines and/or sentences. Remember not all sentences and/or lines will be of equal size. To account for top. Bottom. And seat. Of accumulator. Now simply craft a sentence to tie the various themes, metaphors, sounds and senses of the poem together and *voila!*—you have an entire orgone accumulator! As to care, I'd advise putting the poem in an unused room of the house or apartment—even an enclosed porch or a basement den, as long as the area is dry and well ventilated. And do remember to keep the poem away from sources of electromagnetism or radiation such as TVs, microwaves, cell phones, fluorescent lights, smoke detectors, and nuclear power plants. It is not wise to mess around with a poem that is an orgone accumulator. Now that you've properly located your poem, place yourself in it and reap the benefits of orgone therapy. Have a nice seat. Make yourself comfy. Of course, there are some sacrifices you'll have to make in order to reap said benefits. For instance, while you're sitting in your poem accumulating orgone energy, your poem will not be especially erotic, so you might have to let go of the idea that your poem will someday appear in an anthology of erotic poetry, American or otherwise. Say goodbye to David Lehman, little poem. I myself have been thinking of beginning the Peripatetic School of American Poetry, but it's doubtful I'll be able to launch the school while comfortably seated in this poem. There goes the erotic poem I'd've written about the love I'd be making to my spouse were I not walking in the opposite direction jotting down the love thoughts that came to mind. Oh, you sweet Beverly you. The predicament reminds me of "The Road Not Taken" except that there aren't any diverging roads because we're not going anywhere. No, maybe it reminds me of certain readings of "Prufrock" except that now that I've mentioned Beverly, she's here with me, basking in the blue glow of orgone energy and her spouse's erotic imaginings. "Eeeuw!" she says. Did I mention that the poem is experimental and not a medical device? If you have a medical problem, please consult a health care professional.

*

Think of it as a metaphor if that helps. Or as capital in constant nervous breakdown because under the rule of capital things *must* fall apart. Ghettoes need be and flatscreen TVs. Stately mansions and outside every window the precariat. To market, to market. Somebody's got to be left with nothing but the ability to labor. A lot of somebodies. Next twa corbies wol be sang: "Ye'll sit on his white breast-bane,/ I'll peck out his bonny blue een." "We're all in this together," pundits and politicians proclamate when times get hard. Sure we are. The nation as some godforsaken Trump Tower writ large and we are the average employee. Second class citizens. No black gold. No Texas tea. If it helps, think of it as a metaphor. We're on the *Titanic* and James Cameron, when he's not calling his lead actress "Kate Weighs-a-lot," is directing most of us to the third-class accommodations, where we're meant to fare the worst in case of iceberg. "Never you worry," Captain Cameron says, "Whatever crisis befalls us, it'll just be the tip. Of course, we'll be in a considerably higher and more comfortable quarters than you proverbial riff-raff." But all the waitpersons and other help onboard agree, this is the kind of poem on which you'll see a really big tip. Meanwhile, aware of the women-and-children-first rule, Dubya slips into the Turkish bath to dress himself in something frilly and frivolous. Unfortunately, Barack Obama seems to be half-heartedly helping him on with his girdle. Jefferson Beauregard Sessions III slaps a pacifier in his mouth, slips a bib around his neck, and does his best toddler impersonation. Donald Trump wigs out at Mike Pence, son-in-law Jared, daughter Ivanka, Republican Congress, and alt-right Klan. Paul Ryan prays to Ayn Rand. Then they all golden parachute into lifeboats along with bank CEOs and Wall Street speculators. And lobbyists. Don't forget the lobbyists! Meanwhile, the only way off for the rest of us is via waterboard. Or you can sit here in the accumulator. Alone with your thoughts, like Neil Armstrong walking on the moon and surrounded in the blue light of orgone. When he wasn't yapping into his headset, that is. Like Kate Bush, you can remake the world in your own image. Metamorphose the poem into a cloudbuster. Bring the rain on the rich and the poor alike. The directors and the waterboarded alike. The White Housed and the tent citied alike. The shifty and the truthful. And then let the sun shine. Let the sun shine in. The sun. Shine in.

*

Back in my day, when I wanted some peace and quiet, why, I'd just go hide out in my orgone accumulator. Perch myself on my seatbox, my body less than four inches from the metal inner walls, and leave all my troubles behind. Sometimes I'd bring along my transistor radio and listen to all the hits: "Suite: Judy Blue Eyes," "Ripple," "All Along the Watchtower," "The Ballad of You and Me and Pooneil," "Boulder to Birmingham," "Watching and Waiting." Of course, old Dr. Reich would complain that the transistors and radio waves would play havoc with the precious orgone I'd be supposed to be accumulating, but I always thought the orgone accumulator a peaceful place to develop my musical appreciation—a *locus amoenus* if you will—and besides, I always thought Dr. Reich was speaking figuratively anyway. Or maybe syllogistically. Though much like a poem, an orgone accumulator defies logic. Maybe not in the same way that a poem is able to wander us lonely as a cloud or zero us to the bone or sing us the body electric, but you might notice how orgone energy penetrates everything so that it's unnecessary to undress completely to receive the full benefit. And we got to get ourselves back to the garden. And besides, I always thought Dr. Reich fell behind in his musical appreciation around the time of rama-lama-ding-dong. To this day it's difficult for me to think of the old accumulator without hearing Laura Nyro singing Carole King's "Up on the Roof."

*

A vesicle is an intracellular sac that stores, transports or digests substances within a cell. A fascicle is what scholars have come to call the home-made, hand-sewn volumes of Emily Dickinson's poems. I suppose we could think of the fascicles as transporting down through history the individual poems of Emily Dickinson. A vestibule is an antechamber, hall or lobby next to the outer door of a building. Here's where it gets tricky: if analogies could be drawn from fascicle to vesicle and vesicle to vestibule, then the last of the left-behind ministers of the Kerensky government, hiding out in the vestibule of the Winter Palace might be compared to individual Dickinson poems, say, Minister of Foreign Affairs Terestchenko to "I felt a Funeral, in my Brain," or General Verkovsky, Minister of War, to "Because I could not stop for Death—" but Lenin and Trotsky would probably object that the comparison does a disservice to Dickinson, her poetry being much more bold than any droopy-drawers, mealy-mouthed defenders of capital, probably filled with pusillanimous vesicles besides. And I believe we would have to agree. Fortunately, Wilhelm Reich did not culture vesicles from these gentlemen for his bion experiments of the mid-30s. The vesicles of Reich's experiment gave off a blue glow and observable radiant bioenergy that Reich called orgone, which might be compared not only to the poems in Dickinson's fascicles but also to the inspiration behind the poems. Indeed, the inspiration behind all poems. And if the more or less box shape of this poem on the page could be seen as an orgone accumulator, why, then the US Food and Drug Administration could very likely step in and put the poet in prison. Sorry about that, Emily. Don't worry though, the trustees of Amherst College are still selling tours of your old home and your brother's too. We'll keep reading your poems handed down to us via your fascicles, even though each new editor makes alterations of one kind or another. Speaking of which, doesn't "As imperceptibly as Grief" look a lot groovier with a dash at the end instead of that old period?

*

You might not realize this, but there are not a lot of poets who understand their poems to be orgone accumulators. Even to this day, practitioners of accentual-syllabic verse often misconstrue orgonic rhythmical harmonics as plain old metrical mishigas. Or marsh gas. For, while you can count stresses or syllables or words per line, the orgone energy pulsing through a particular poem defies precise measurement. Not that the accentual-syllabic stuff is for the birds, but nine and fifty swans, one nightingale, a raven, an eagle, a blur where once was a hummingbird, and a very few birds coming back, one or two, and you misconstrue the components of the poem for its pizzazz, all mixed up like Melanie Daniels sitting on the bench outside the Bodega Bay elementary school telling herself she enjoys hearing the children sing but every once in a while looking over her shoulder at the monkey bars and, you know, counting. You'd think free verse or open field or organic form poets would do better, but they confuse the "Brownian movement" that Einstein utilized to explain away the rise in temperature inside the accumulator with the hand-me-down "Browning moment" of their narrators' first-person observations. You see, it's all about how the random movement of microscopic particles suspended in a liquid or gas make it difficult to find one's own voice. I don't know, maybe you could find a prose poet or two who might have a clue. Anyway, it may come as a surprise then that there's a story—one I'll admit might be apocryphal—that the first FDA officials who arrived on the scene to destroy Wilhelm Reich's orgone accumulators and burn his books couldn't complete their job. They got the book bonfire going alright, but when the pair took a gander at the accumulators lined up one next to the other, the one said to the other, "Reminds me of poetry." And the second agent said, "I think that I shall never see . . ." and his voice sort of trailed off into a mumble that didn't rhyme or even scan very well and sounded a little like "-mulator" at the end. Did I say there was a story? I meant a narrative poem. Or a poem en prose in any event. I can't say for sure that it's narrative in the sense that you'd normally think of when you use the term. Or do you say "utilize"? If you do, why? You know, *normal*, like beginning, middle and . . . Anyway, it might be apocryphal. Or apocalyptical? There were birds in the sky. Or just some random anecdote. But I never saw them winging. That I shall never see. No, I never saw them at all . . .

*

Blue Moon
You left me standing en poem
Like that first man on the moon
In the blue light
of orgone

We Each Fertilize Our Own Straw Bale

For Mike Barrett

I feel pretty okay now the building's empty. Kinda damp though. What's that about? Bartleby's "NO" to the not-NO the kid quits on in "A&P," and I'm remembering I was like, Well, hush my mouth and call me frankly, have you ever felt the power of the state? Tear gas? Bus ride with bars on the windows? Stand in a prison yard munching on bologna on Wonder Bread with a paper cuppa Kool-Aid? Fucking Ezra Pound gets a goddess when he's in a cage in Italy. I'm sharing a big dorm room with a bunch of guys and Allen Ginsberg. Yeah, om. But what if "time" is nothing more than misrecognized change? And say war is the spirit of our times: Christians would choke; Jihadis puke. We're always killing the wrong people in wars. My knees *are* arthritic. How'd you know? Hard to stand to be part of a wave, so I'm glad we don't do that at Wrigley. Pragmatic prophets: were there ever any? Tell you a secret I learned after the tear gas. There are thirty million stories in the naked polis, and this secret will have been one of them: negative not-negative capability. Don't ask, maybe I won't tell. How the neutrinos got into the dead star. Why meaning is always darker in the morning. Okay, so the place is kinda like an empty tomb. Imagine a dank, damp garden. No, no way a whole legion fits into this self we got here. That exorcism where the cohort of pigs went jumping off the cliff? Jesus thought they were lemmings. Internationals: First (disbanded by battles with anarchists, numbered thereafter), Second (WWI and done, everyone killing the wrong persons), Third (gulags and show trials and bears, oh my), Fourth (WWII and ka-poo, neoconservatives come after), Fifth (yeah, good luck). A half century, God bless. But you'll have to make *poiein* suffice. Or sacrifice. Look out the window and tell me you know that's not the Tree of Life. On second thought: Green Gus woke up, blinked, abstracted by the past. Remembered Jung's Anti-Semitism, and Ford's: *The Dearborn Independent*. Remember: if it's one, you can be a devil, hot stuff. Not the same drowsy truth, never mind the movie violence. I am a fortified hacienda, not a sexual dungeon. You go for the popcorn, not-me. The sociopath writes and writes in notebook after notebook: all the ideas, the fantasies, the not-fantasies, the physics problems. Exponential decay and old man smell. Dark and damp, you'd imagine (not-imagine, rather). By the time of the index, he spoke before the commencement and was threatened by some who watched Fox News. Was crucified, died, and was buried. Passively constructed. Blue Suede Shoes. Class in a class house. Blood dis-solves, un-solves, like the opening paragraph in one of those detective stories by Hector Aaron Poole. In a movie about the oil fires in Iraq, fondly remembered poverty, and they wondered what they would use to remember "anthropocentric." Not knock-knock jokes. Not thrum of traffic. Neither sufficient reason nor the Mississippi River. Spinoza demands, "Not the principle of sufficient reason?!!" Which class in the class house was a dick, and which was a friend? During his sermon, the priest said, "We must get behind the president in Vietnam," and on the way home, I had a bad taste, complex but dark. Laura Nyro sang, "Captain St. Lucifer." Soon enough, eyes were not drying, even in the sun. Far from my father, in the twenty-first century, I recall thinking how old I would be by 2000. Farther from my father; farther also from the cosmic frog. Pigeons coo at the window; we two in each other's arms. Benjaminian nostalgia/ not-nostalgia. Sufficient reason walked up to the world and said, "Now we can sort things out." You are a man green with wisdom (meant as a complement). The iron-booted heels of interest with an interest in eternity. Can ego leave out the "the"? Facts stick to me like an ambulance siren approaching from the east. Make no mistake: a cosmic frog needs no pond. The labor of our silence is, rather than the value of our labor. He hurtled down the cliff face at speeds of 40 mph, recording all with his beautiful headcam. All along, I have been a group of people banded together and treated as a group. Either that or a group of people with a common statistical characteristic. (How I recall looking in the mirror before the orals for my PhD and thinking, "Five of them and me—they're outnumbered three to one.") I must've figured I was not too short to mythologize myself. When I'd open the window, our dog Sam would sniff in the pee-drippled, wind-luscioused, rabbit-tousled world. It calmed me when the situation was complicated, or the bottom rode low. This kingdom, self-consciousness—once kingdom of bug. I had stormed earlier that the river of time could not be forked. Those younger days when I believed I would see St. Francis on the subway, bent slightly sideways by his hemp shoulder bag, from which a four-month-old black lab peeks. A jury of black bears listen to the grizzly prosecutor growling out the charges against Betsy DeVos. Humble enough, we require an absorption of heat. Almost remembered marching uniform blue in the Union Army—one life lived in the proud 54th. Now I lay me down my egg/I pray to totems night and day/If I return into my head/ Leviathan will swim away. No point: nothing is as nothing doing. Frank agrees about forgiveness—and the time to transcend capital. If the market crashed in the woods without even a black bear around to hear it, would the vulture hedge funds still descend? "You were horny for a loaf, you lug nut!" In some Heideggerian romance in an empty building, Hector Aaron Poole pelted my paintings with his own sex and swastikas, but I wasn't married to them anyway. Soon, with conflict, my life improved. And I remembered, "Every mechanical refrigeration system operates at two different pressure levels," but do not be afraid to call someone when the water heater breaks down. "Knock-knock" "Who's there?" "*Ex*" "*Ex* who?" '*Ex nihilo*" "Who?" Christ was satire: the ride into Jerusalem on the mule a parody of a Roman Triumph. Christ was a good egg, could appreciate a good come-back. When he holds a world in each hand, you got your compliment and your complement. Put plants in it, and the fertilized straw bale will grow them well until the cold cutting winds of fall calls on my mother and sister to pull them or cut them down and carry them inside against those northerly winds and of all God's creation. Joe and I would take our dirty clothes to the laundromat together—sorting clothes, pouring in detergent, never dreaming we'd be so farther away in time. Social networks and screenshots will never find him. Everybody happens according to ideology. God bless the border collie *arr arr*, the borador *roowf roowf*, and the German shepherd mix *rarr rarr*. Good dogs, good dogs (perhaps this is a prayer). (The prayer.) Little Shamey's ears were so big, one folded over for months. What have I unread upon my bookshelves? More than I be able to scale, dear axons. Looking for an honest concupiscent man. In the face of adultery, who gives a fuck about Satan? The "ayes" have it, which grow out of the brain. Get thee behind me, president in Vietnam! "Why should we live guilt?" the clay people ask Flash Gordon. Morning light, Mom's garden, Baltimore orioles in flight: all caught through picture window. Laura Nyro sings, "Time and Love." Sun waving all afternoon. And tell me how it is in the brain, to bang out a dent. Truth is, all arguments are *ex nihilo.* Robert Johnson was wary of the planets, their retrograde motions. Green Heinekens are wearing down my bones with time and old man smell. And what kind of soup are we in with mother in every cell and father in Hell, obviously not in Hell? We are Christmas fruitcakes and Kierkegaardian dangles; we are concupiscent orioles and naked buildings; lovers of the concrete drainage ditch and empty polis or the rest in deep winter. And the rest flew in the direction of the morning star, like time and tear gas. James G. Blaine Elementary School, where the rabble-rouser principal was let go. Fossil fuel rot, flatten out over this one lived. Raven out the window takes to flight black with glint of purple like metamorphic rock. Barbed wire for private property. Glad they don't do that now the building's empty. We all have our entropies. Redbud tree in our yard where the pear used to be. Beverly and I sit out there—cold beer after cold beer. Tall brown grass. Dogs lie nearby on cement. I remember Laura Nyro sang, "Brown Earth."

Just Like *Volume Two*

Also for Mike Barrett

"Morning came to the windows/in the street/selling red watermelons," sings Laura Nyro, "five cents apiece." The Tokyo markets may open or not, but trust the farm report for apple futures, tomato futures. Chicago River used to smell of chemicals and God knows what all, but now it's returned to life and green every St. Patrick's Day. Industry's gone. Now funding for schools—K through 12, public universities. Scientists named the Hadean Eon after the Greek God Hades. Methanogen State Park where the last ride is Deoxyribonucleic. *Volume Two*, just like Soft Machine. "Pataphysical Introduction": something in the motion of the rabbit Sammy fancied, caused him to tug on the leash. Imagine grading cohort for a grade. If I were a better doggy daddy, I'd explain to Sam and Jasmine and Seamus that they are all, each one of them, an exception, and I'm studying them as they teach me. Can you believe we all look so much alike? We are all drivers on the ice glaze going 50 mph, moving into a spin, and if we just let go, listen to Laura Nyro's "Brown Earth"—such an accurate measure of creation. "Trump U," the school's own brochure called it. The concise British alphabet: *abcdefghijklmnopqrstuvwxyz, ahem, ahem.* Water dripping from the brim of his hat, making hyrdoglyphs on the rug as he walks along the corridor looking for the gumshoe's office, but the lettering on the frosted glass of the doors is none too helpful: if it's not *Commune of Women Foreseers*, it's *Order of Ventricle Symmetry*; if it's not *Board of the College of Pataphysics*, then it's *endowment for entropy.* He's mumbling, "seventy times blue heaven hawk, and every forty yards some pseudo-random rock." How can dualism reign? "Got me," answered and ran he out in the cold rain and snow. Kleptocrat national news cohorts all reporting the same I've-met-Him psychosis. Out of the hyperbolic frying pan and into what would be the proverbial pataphor. Out of the blue will come spirits. Cold warrior counter-revolutionary aesthetics: mud and chicken/ shit upon//an upside down/wheelbarrow// not so red sitting/in a muddy puddle. Look backwards at failing material. *I been shavin' mah face since the time I was ten/ Gimme a razor and I'll shave it again/ 'cause I'm a Man/ M-A-N-N-N!* Essence or presence; nurture or nuclear. What do we do about the radioactive goo coming out through the crack in the mud house floor? Doubt is a fraction of Cartesian reaction. The Hackensack turtle above the water lizard sits in the palm of my frontal lobe—watch out for the droll drilling! It's pretty much a proverbial businessman's trip to the portal of Judeo-Christianity. *Marx and Moses sittin' in a tree . . .* Imagine a humble bed. This patient, humble bed. Humble like cephalochordates, vaguely fish-shaped, lacking brain, clearly defined heads, and sense organs. Talk about the patience: Baruch/ Benedictus/Bento Spinoza waited to publish until, hypothetically, the bony plates of all the huge-boned creeds were unearthed. He moves towards the last door down the lonely corridor, feeling like a monad already, and there he discerns: *Hector Aaron Poole, P.I.* Then it's Old Ezra at the Universidad de Cuidad Jaurez, political rube in Milton Freidman sheepskin, wondering, "IED wounds or H.D. wounds?" Holy Ghost or Great White Swale? As if to identify, almost, Christ's pastoralized quadriceps all over the American

West. And the hamburger joints, if you don't mind my beside-the-point. Heretical boob in button-down shirt, denim shorts, purple cape and pointy beard wants to complain that the left brain Sapphos while the right brain Adornos. I lost my wedding ring all that weather ago and walked the dogs out in the snow—white pain—heartbroken and wondering what I'd lose next. Compliance department: We are but creatures of gravity, nucleons, and *ahem, ahem, zyxwvutsrqponmlkjihgfedcba.* We are but Polish nuns fighting off Nazis in a neighborhood department store where that mother of mine worked and worked and became assistant supervisor with a five-cent raise. When your sense of history, you could cut, sand, stain, and reassemble, and still it'd be "Did you get a raise?" "Five cents." The historian does not even call them plantations: "They are slave labor camps." Eden always leaving, we are but come from transideological beginnings. She never pataphor she didn't cake. She made such an odd work of it. Cold garden, cold flies and then the half-dead tree of knowledge and a hypertext reference to Hades or a concentration camp or nowhere. Asked me about the south winter stars while walking above the old bird branches. *Swallows swallows.* We need denial of binary opposition (bitter pill). Pancras with a head for faith > Pancras without a head for faith. The half living tree of knowledge, you know? When the aliens came, nobody believed them. I visited Barronett, Wisconsin, and saw Baltimore orioles. Swallows follow fallow fields; fellow swallows swallow dark energy. Two opposed to *dicht*: did you mean *dight*? Did you mean *ditto*? They were miners for monads until the canary caught a migraine; they were minors with migraines caught in a cannery looking to be monads. Here's a golden oldie from Godel, one of my faves: "When in fiction the city becomes a character, it is not the only character in fiction we have read or will read, but don't be surprised if city hall is a kidney." And a golden oldie from Fibonacci is the pattern 1 1 2 3 5 8 and so on and so on including the previous and so on. The Subaru Service Department has Buddha nature? What is your car smoking? We live in denial of binary opposition (a single set of unpaired chromosomes). The way through Manicheanism is the three-in-one God, like a Swiss Army Knife, be sure to take it with you if before the start of Fall semester—back to cohort away from cohort—you're up on the Sawatch Mountains. There's Pops looking down through the gray clouds and pinetops of the watching forest as Sonny hops, skips and jumps haploidily along, and finally the indivisible light through the trees not represented by any map. What are we but unused plank-roofed playhouses whose broken rope ladders no one any longer wants to climb? Just like Soft Machine: "Have You Ever Bean Green?" Seems like just a microcentury ago and an altoparsec away and now we are had-beans. In the annals of agnotology, Descartes' place is doubtful. Winter afternoon and Jasmine watches longingly the squirrel jump up the ice-glazed side of the garage and then slowly begin to slide down. Laura Nyro sang, "Well, I've got a lot of patience, baby/ And that's a lot of patience to lose/ I'm crying, I'm mad at my country . . ." In Arkansas standing water *Naegleria fowleri*; in Louisiana's drinking water *Naegleria fowleri*. Camping with the dogs, we find Jasmine understands well the zipper and can open the tent in the night; she can find the power bars in Beverly's backpack. Individual poems in their several cohorts in their binary volumes, unopposed. Your grandmother at the Eastland

Boat Disaster; my great-grandmother at the Great Chicago Fire. To ornithology there's no true ontology—you have to wing it. Dust corn brown/ dried of futures hard/ sky empty & air/ from heat out /pulls drought. Who drains all this energy? Malignant narcissist capital. That is nothing but what can only be. Until we find that corner and deduct ourselves. Among the salmon-colored rocks and sunlight, this one life.

Mark Rothko's *Subway*

You might think it's a perfect example of Depression Era art, but no, it's already the next century and we're still waiting here at this subway stop. Fuckin' a, take the A train. People are pretty thin, you think, like they've been eating in soup kitchens, but that's just anorexia. Or bulimia. We got all kindsa body image dysmorphia down here, so get over it. I got a couple colors in my head. Maybe three. We're hoping the fast food munching crowd doesn't arrive before the train does. It gets pretty tight, what with the bodies pressed together and the tossed remnants of buffalo wings and bacon cheese burgers. And the processed murdered meat smell. It's no *Garden of Earthly Delights*, let me tell you. But who'd want that anyway? How do people get around that center panel without the subway? You have to learn to ride unicorns or wildebeests. And with my luck, I'd end up in the panel on the right. Stuck inside a bird mouth with Chicago blues again. With a coupla colors stickin' in my head, like a melody I don't even know if I like. Remember the old days when Karl Marx thought that alienation would be the inevitable result of capitalism? At least down here with Rothko if anything really bad happens, you can hide behind a pillar. Or maybe keep your nose in your newspaper. Probably the best way to stay away from bad news. Never did report on the secret first meeting of the Mont Pelerin Society, nor on the truth of trickle-down economics. Never did question a government foreign policy of preventative Blitzkrieg. Just downright confusing about Trump and his Russian pals. And all of Trump's all of a sudden Republican

Party pals, meaning almost all the godforsaken Republicans. Meaning we're downright satisfied with two all-beef patties and two political parties. Alienation has been preserved and changed and exchanged. Each person alone behind a newspaper or a pillar or their thoughts. They are metaphors for cell phones. Not the thoughts, the pillars and newspapers. Or maybe metonymy. Which is why the painting is actually called *Untitled*. And why *Subway* is enclosed in parentheses. No, it's not about the crappy fast food chain. It's Rothko's version of maybe Hell. And, well, thanks to capitalism, one of my many versions of Hell. No exits and all. But we'd rather be down here than in Heaven, Beverly, what with what U.S. Christians are calling their God these days. Believe me, Jesus prefers it here too. Shaking his head, talking to himself, "Just because I said the poor will always be with you didn't mean go ahead and make up some cockamamie economic theory to more drastically impoverish . . ." The colors in my head and the place where those different colors come together. At the station here those different colors come together. Actually, he's not right here with us yet. He's scheduled to come by and harrow the place one more time, and the colors in my head, only he's at the 59th street station with a broke-down train that'll probably take an eternity to fix. Just kidding. The train's bringing the next major depression, and, from the tremors and the light down the tunnel and the hole in the ground we've been in for almost always already, I'd say it's right on time.

Certain Curious Proclivities Abide Amidst the Post-Bride Mountainside Laboratory-Hideaway

"Don't touch that leever!" cries Doctor Pretorius, by which he means the lever handily installed in many a standard mad science laboratory scenically sited upon mountaintop so said laboratory and mountain can be conveniently blown to smithereens should experimental outcomes require a drastic drawing board revision on account of what scientists with their penchant for Latinate-dominated vocabulary term "humungous snafus," or should the plot become too improbable for suspension of disbelief, or say if somebody's feelings get hurt, which is our predicament since the would-be bride, who quite resembles Mary Shelley, if you recall, screeches and hisses each time the monster approaches, whereupon he grabs hold the aforementioned lever, demands Henry and Elizabeth "Go!" and "Live!" and proceeds with vigorous downward thrust. Henry and Elizabeth skedaddle and the film screen rattles with the force of several blasts whilst what looks like umpteen thousand bucketloads of one-time mountainside (i.e., dirt) spatters at the viewers who leave the theater at the first sign of THE END, as unbeknownst to them, the castle-laboratory survives! as do those inside! though now after bumpity ride and perilous slide pitched a bit precariously upon what remains of the mountain. "I specifically asked you not to mess with that thing," Pretorius reprimands. "I'm *trying* to build you a lovely bride!" Sparks spit over his left shoulder from hiccupping lab equipment. *"She hate me,"* the monster replies, and the bride obliges with another hiss as Minnie arrives, takes a gander around the lab, screams and faints. Unperturbed, Pretorius looks down his nose from the dead-to-the-world woman to the other-worldly undead one, then resumes, "She's only the *first*. Everyone who's anyone has trouble with the first. Why, even T. S. Eliot had problems with his first wife. It's not so serious as all that, doesn't have to be love 'er and leever. I'll make you a better wife." The indignant ex-bride hisses at the mad scientist, who glares at her. *"Not wife,"* says the monster. *"Make me Ezra Pound."* Flabbergasted, Pretorius replies, "Pound?!! O, *monstrosa aesthetica conceptio*! What do you want with an Ezra Pound? He's all: 'Make it new! Make it new!' and then it's antique language, musty books, centuries-dead poetical concerns." *"I . . . like centuries dead."* "Yes. And why am I not astonished?" *"Him nice to Eliot. Not hiss . . . like her,"* and he points at the ex, who screeches and exits the scorched hole where door once fit. Meanwhile, Pretorius rolls his eyes, shakes his head, tries again, "Eliot wrote *The Waste Land*." *"I like . . . Waste Land."* "Yes, yes, so you do. 'I had not thought death had undone so many' 'jug-jug, twit-twit,' yatta-yatta. Well, Pound just edited." *"Oh."* "Besides, he couldn't even make his own work cohere!" *"Cohere bad!"* "Alright! Alright!" Pretorius relents while Minnie awakens and asks, "Pree-tor-ius? What kind of name is Pree-tor-ius?" "Oh, Moddish," he replies. "Go-go boots, paisley scarves and all?" "Quite. Nehru jackets and bellbottoms too. Why don't you go fetch yours and we'll have a nice night on the town." "Oh, lovely!" Minnie enthuses and disappears through the hellhole. Pretorius smiles after her, "*Voila!* Sometimes my powers of, oh, let's say prestidigitation amuse even myself." The monster asks, *"How make Pound? Unbury dead? Find poet brain?"* Secret gaiety lights Pretorius's eyes as he murmurs, "And where would we *ever* happen upon gray matter for Mr. 'Brain's-a-great-clot-of-genital-fluid'?" Then shakes his head, "No. Not *find*, my dear fellow. Rather I have shored up my peculiarities against a time such as this. *Your* brain I grew from seed. Our Pound will have to grow from a nut." The monster furrows his brow, *"Him stand in wood. Him be tree."* "Precisely! I give him life and a friendly critique of his early lines." *"Critique bad!"* and the monster looms menacingly. "Perhaps," Pretorius says, backing toward the exit, "a nice night on the town with Minnie's just what this otherwise-strangely-unavailable-to-women doctor ordered." The monster advances circuitously through ruined gurneys and operating table, worse-for-wear laboratory furnishings and battered electrical equipment, spattering sparks, overturned medical carts, much bestrewn and ill-used forceps, hemostats, scalpels, electric drills and bone saws, charred anatomical charts, broken beakers, tossed test tubes, shattered specimen jars, smashed syringes, water-damaged forbidden books, and one worse-for-wear theremin. "*Sacrum, sacrum, iluminatio coitu,*" intones the mad scientist as our plot wanders, at first over the cervical ganglion, then augmenting into medulla oblongata, cerebellum and cerebrum when Karl (the lab assistant whom you might assume would be named Igor—pronounced *eee-gor* or even *eye-gor*—but assumptions make bumpkins of local villagers and mad scientist matchmakers alike) climbs through the one-time doorway having lately taken a spill and looking a bit weather-beaten and, well, monster-beaten. "Let me just interject at this point," he says. "Teasing that big palooka's pretty much like playing with fire." As the monster lumbers after Pretorius, Karl pauses, glances around the lab and asks, "Where's Elizabeth? I so had my heart set on her."

Theodicy

No, not *The Odyssey*. We're not following Odysseus around recording his adventures. It's more like we're following God around, as would Gottfried Wilhelm Leibniz, cleaning up after him—kinda like David Hume except with a vacuum cleaner. And while it may seem today an oddity about our philosophical forefathers' theodicies—how Adam and Eve weren't married, ran around the garden in their altogether smoking dope listening to rock music and making love and not a peep out of God, but like about five minutes later He's raining down fire and brimstone on Sodom and Gomorrah and turning people's wives into pillars of salt, for crying out loud, and next things we know, we're deciding distinctions between venial and mortal sins, natural and moral evils, serial and spree killers, and who can blame us for our second guesses or various and Sunday looks askance?—Leibniz wouldn't have been doing any such questioning, for he was certain that just as soon as enough Newtons showed up, whatsoever metaphysical conundrum would become quite clear. No, it was David Hume who set out to make dicey theodicy-making. Let's see, how many Newtons does it take to screw in God's lightbulb? Why did the logical positivists cross the road? Because Wittgenstein did. But they failed to watch for traffic. Ouch, Vienna can be cruel between the wars. And wear army boots with iron heels. March, march, march: are you sure they're not following Odysseus around? The sleep of reason is supposed to produce monsters, but you put your head down on the pillow and, by Goya, the damn bedroom fills with bats and owls. Well, them and Nazis. Who reasoned like demons. Which casts some doubt on the whole twentieth-century project of trying to take God out of the theodicy. Hence, right-wing fundamentalists rely on faith and grace to put the *mean* back in meaningful relationship to Christ. Yet when Barton Fink asks the elevator man if he's read the Bible, Pete replies, "I've heard of it." Madman Mundt—did I say "mad man"? People can be so cruel, and Vienna between the wars—Mundt says, "Where there's a head there's hope," and I don't think Descartes could've put it any better. Of course, Mundt does also say, "Heil Hitler!" and shotguns the cop's brains all down the hotel corridor. But we were talking about Leibniz anyway. So it seems the paradox is between whether God's all-powerful or all-good. Or is that the corporation? Well, whatever allows lobbyists, fundamentalist mega-preachers, and politicians to put the *me* back in meaningful relationship to Christ. We *do* know that had Friedrich Nietzsche been a poet, he'd've said, "Whatever does not kill me makes me firmer of line and nearer of rhyme." And yet we are haunted by what we cannot synthesize: the uncanny resemblance between Georg Wilhelm Friedrich Hegel and Jacob Marley. You realize, of course, that if we were following Odysseus around, we'd've made a lot more progress: by now his crew would be transmogrified into pigs or wombats or whatever and our hero would be having slurpy sex with Circe the sorceress. "Satisfied?" she would ask, steam rising from both their bodies. Odysseus would smile contentedly. Outside, the hoots and giggles of wombats.

Armed Teachers [with Mental Illness]

"Good morning class. Whoops! Forgot my gun today. Can anybody lend me one of theirs?" No, this is not about Salt Lake City, Utah, where the elementary school teacher shot herself in the faculty restroom. That is, in the leg. In the faculty restroom. Unaware of her concealed carry permit, the toilet was sneaking up behind her. BLAMMO!! Nor does this concern the Crystal River, Florida, social studies teacher who, as a white nationalist, ran a regular podcast and also complained on Twitter about being able to "literally feel brain cells dying" because she's "forced to learn about institutional racism." Right, why rely on impersonal institutions when you can give racism your own unique individual stamp. That's what neoliberal economists and Republican and New Democratic politicians call "taking personal responsibility!" These incidents do not stop Orange 45 from doubling down after he changed his mind all around on what to do about school shootings. So, I'm preparing for class tomorrow at the rifle range. Empty a magazine, go over my lesson plans, maybe go have a few beers, empty another magazine, maybe grade a few papers, and head home. Start the semester right: school supplies—grade book, #2 pencils, low-odor dry-erase markers, guns and ammo. It'll be rootin' tootin' straight-shootin' off to teach readin' writin' 'rithmetics and rapid-firin'. So this wouldn't concern, for example, the Virginia teacher who fired blanks at his students. BLAMMO!! BLAM!!! BLAMMO!! He didn't have to repeat "Class Dismissed." Or Georgia's Dalton High School teacher—social studies again!—who locked himself alone in his classroom and fired out the window. BLAMMO! Just two meetings with the NRA after he accused Republican senators of being afraid of the NRA, and the orange one's looking a lighter shade of yellow. But, you know what Robert Reich advises, "Focus on his policies—not his orange-ness and mental state." Yeah, good luck with separating the two. Feeling bilious this morning? Start a trade war, let Gary Cohn walk away. (Gary's not worried—he's Goldman Sachs and they got their big tax break.) Last night's last Big Mac didn't sit right? Fire Rex Tillerson for putting Putin in a bad light. Imagine the benefits of armed teachers for the math class: "Okay, class, I've got six magazines, three of which hold twenty rounds, two of which hold thirty-five, and one I've just emptied into the neo-Nazi shooter who is full of about four pounds of lead. How many total rounds did I start out with this morning?" And for those K-12 public schools that still have Geography class: no more old-fashioned wooden pointers or even new-fangled laser pointers. We aim our trusty AR-15 and blast the targeted nation. Some of us like to play "The Star-Spangled Banner" too. Prepares the kids for their future in the military or law enforcement, just as school choice prepares them for their post-graduation choice: working for less than minimum wage or prison. You know how Michelle Obama says, "When they go low, we go high"? Well, we armed teachers with mental illness, we target the heart or the head. None of this silly making people dance for us. Not during class time. We've got a lesson plan and we are gonna stick to it.

> It was over in a moment
> And the students gathered round
> There before them lay the body

Of the shooter on the ground

Oh, he might have went on living

But he made one fatal slip

When he tried to match the adjunct

With the big iron on his hip

Big iron on his hip

But at the university level? Adjuncts will have it the hardest. Without a private office of their own. Slinging the weaponry to school and back, I gotta tell you, it's hell. But it's an All-American kind of hell, if you get my figurative language and my fair and balanced, serve and protect, instruction and destruction, with us or against us, *pro patria et momento mori*, dungeons or dragons, one lump or two, tune in, turn on, flower power, give peace a chance or we all shine on, we are stardust or we are golden, cops and Klan work hand in hand, guns don't kill dinosaurs, dinosaurs kill dinosaurs, the NRA kills children kind of thinking as we slide, well-armed, from the proletariat to the precariat. But you know what Robert Reich says, "Remember this is a regime and he is not acting alone." That's a big 10-4. Health care out the window and tax breaks for the elite and the affluent and wealthy and the well-to-do and the opulent and the 1% and the loaded and the rolling in dough and the denizens of 740 Park Avenue and the affluenzaed, and the filthy, stinking, verminous, virulent, gluttonous, sociopathic, malevolent rich. And yet—upset that General Kelly has downgraded Jared Kushner's security clearance to "can read only the Entertainments sections of newspapers"?—President Orange slams the breaks on Broadcom's $117 billion bid to buy up Qualcomm and tells the generals, "You're fired!" And pretty much by himself overturns any decent thing former President Obama did, including that deal about trying to keep certain mentally ill people away from weapons of messy destruction. Very few janitorial and housekeeping staff are left these days, and one doing the work of umpteen. My advice, leave a tip. You never know who's wearing a concealed carry. Coming spring break: a week to sit on the beach with those strawberry coladas and margaritas, while we clean and oil our pieces. Then it's back to school and now where did I put those grenades? But the Orange Balloon did not act alone when he answered the problem of mass shootings in schools. Nope, lotsa help from the NRA and Republican Congress. The stategy is: got a problem? Throw guns at it! Worked in Vietnam and Korea—where it might well work again!—and greatly aided Mexico with their War on Drugs, which the US forced on them. Worked in Afghanistan, Iraq, Syria, Libya, Mali, Yemen, the South Sudan, places our students can't even find on a map—because we're teaching to the test! No world geography! No civics classes either! Luckily, we responsible teachers with mental illnesses are packing. Not the Florida teacher with the white supremacist dating advice and the rapid-fire racial slurs. Or the math instructor in Little Springs, Georgia, who was probably trying to kill himself. BLAMMO! He couldn't hit the broad side of a toilet. No, he wasn't trying to avoid teaching his class about institutional racism. The good news is there are fewer white supremacist teachers than white supremacist police or border patrol or military personnel. Of course, that's also the bad news. Nor is this about the Seaside, California, teacher who fired his gun at the ceiling and injured a student with falling debris. BLAMMO! The kid's lucky a toilet from the faculty restroom above didn't fall on him. Turns out those Robert Reich rules were misattributed anyway. Next Tuesday's composition class: "Now remember, class, a magazine holds shells under spring pressure in preparation for feeding into the firearm's chamber. Examples include box, tubular, drum and rotary magazines. Some are fixed to the firearm, like this one here, while others are removable, like the six on the desk at the back of the room. All of this will be on the test." And still—Robert Mueller closing in? James Comey going public with possible *kompromat*—meaning "compromising material," meaning Russian prostitutes and golden showers? Fire missiles at Syria! Pick Twitter fights with Putin! Try to crawl back to the TPP! (Pee pee?) (The great negotiator in the Russian hotel: "Let's play, 'I represent a great nation, and you're a nation, too.'") No, this is not about the Marjory Stoneman Douglas chemistry teacher and volunteer class gun-toter who left his loaded Glock 9 millimeter handgun in a Men's room stall at the beach for some drunk to find and— BLAMMO!!—what is it about teachers with guns in bathroom stalls? "'Have gun, will travel's' the CV of a teach/ with #2 pencils and lead mass shooters eat." Nor the gotta-get-off-my-sore-feet, underpaid, and less-than-vigilant resource officer whose gun was fired—BLAMMO!—while still holstered, thanks to a third-grade wiseguy. But I wouldn't go blaming the insufficiently remunerated resource officer at Stoneman Douglas High in Parkland, Florida, for not going up against an AR-15 with a lousy handgun. The solution is obvious: teachers in tanks! Teachers with bazookas, grenades, AK-47s, AR-15s, rocket launchers, heat-seeking missiles, weaponized drones, nuclear arsenals. Call them weapons of mass education. But wait! If it's misattributed, how do we know what

Robert Reich said? Is he a bot? But imagine the nightmares! Betsy DeVos: after a difficult day of avoiding public schools in urban areas, encouraging legislation to break teachers' unions and hold down salaries, and seeking spiritual pathways to subvert Title IX, dreams of armed teachers stealing her family's nine yachts and turning them into floating grammar schools for inner-city kids. Paul Ryan dreams he's hiding behind his hardcover signed copy of Ayn Rand's *Atlas Shrugged* when the red-state teachers arrive—fully locked and loaded, full metal jacketed, Ramboed and GI Joed of whatever gender—and invite him to "show us your inventive little Personal Responsibility Two-Step, Paul." BLAM! BLAMMETTY! In Marco Rubio's nightmare, they're Florida teachers, and they demand, "C'mon, Marco, you danced around Parkland survivor Cameron Kasky's questions about refusing NRA money; how about you dance around a few dozen rounds." BLAMMO!! BLAMMETTY! BLAM! Meanwhile Mitch McConnell envisions Kentucky teachers calling him "Old Turtle Head" and reminding him that he's one of the wealthiest senators while their state is one of the poorest. Then he's shelled. In Supreme Court dreams— BLAM!! BLAMMETTY!! BLAM!!—it's the Gorsuch Hop, the Roberts Twist and Shout, the Alito Fleeto-Feeto, the Pube-in-My-Coke-Can Thomas Stomp, and The Off-Kilter Kavanaugh Cocky Walk. And Donald Trump's nightmares are the worst: red and blue state adjunct instructors teach him a lesson.

Search Me, Little Varmints

Just one look out the door and you know it's not the Seekers, the 1960s pop group that sang about Georgy Girl who'd be "swinging down the street so fancy free" and "window shopping but never stopping to buy" before she was apparently kidnapped by "Comanch," as Ethan Edwards would say. He wouldn't sing along with the others. He'd sort of mumble and mark time. And little Francis smelling napalm, and little George seeing fascist stormtroopers from outer space, and little Stephen wishing she had shed her dowdy feathers and flown on a bicycle with a cuddly alien friend, and little Marty smiling when Ethan and his nephew come upon the body of Georgy Girl's sister. The body's not quite on screen and little Marty says, "Here's a leg. Here's a wing," never stopping to think that the film's kidnap/miscegenation concern might be a metaphor for a more immediate mainstream American fear: the nightmare of a March on Washington for civil rights and all the white women kidnapped by A. Phillip Randolph's Brotherhood of Sleeping Car Porters. Next thing, you might find that Mamie Eisenhower wants to stay in the African American community, even if she has to live in public housing. "Aye and begumption," says local law enforcement. "This is just like the time Marian Anderson made off with Eleanor Roosevelt and wouldn't let her go home until she quit the Daughters of the American Revolution." Meanwhile, John Wayne, Ward Bond, and John Ford do all that they can to assist the rescue—cussin' and wavin' the red, white and blue, and throwing authentic-looking stunt punches.

Ronald Reagan had so hoped to be invited to join the posse chasing after Marian Anderson's Comanches, but nobody bought his cowboy routine—what with the ten-gallon hat, the football, and the monkey—so he has to settle for testifying as a friendly witness before the House Un-American Activities Committee, twirling a lasso and turning in long lists of Actors' Guild members. The Hollywood Ten are off to prison and little Marty responds, "Who wants a wing?" And year after year Ethan Edwards and his one-eighth-Indian, thoroughly assimilated nephew Martin search for the missing kidnap victim, calling out, "Hey There! Georgy Girl!" and spend their evenings by the campfire with the nephew reading to Ethan dead animal poems, aromatic of citizenly concern while pretty much through a glass darkly about the Cold War or wacky Edward Teller's hydrogen bomb or the electrocution of the Rosenbergs or the red-baiting assault on the unions and the civil rights movement or the murder of Emmett Till. The concern goes right over Ethan's head, but he so enjoys the carnage. He has Martin read over and over Osborne Obstreperowski's poems "Red Squirrel in My Headlights" ("Squish!" Ethan guffaws), "Parakeet Deceased Owing to a Plummet into the Pepper Pot Soup" ("Mmm-mmm, Good!" Ethan snortles), and "Still Life With Lawn Mower and Stilled Life" ("Ekk-frrastick!" Ethan guffortles). Meanwhile, little Marty envisions a Greek chorus of Joe McCarthys chanting at the conclusion of each poem an antistrophic, "Who wants a wing?" And yet, unlike many dead animal poets, the road to publication for the young Osborne Obstreperowski had been early bestrewn and blockaded by the carcasses of poems criticized and rejected. Indeed, his immediate post-war deceased animal poem, "Dead Elephant in the Living Room of Berlin" struck his New Critical mentor and editor of a famous poetry magazine, Stanley Crowe Tater, as "sentimental" in its suggestion that Hitler's Germany might be considered not a roadside ditch but rather a necessary swerve along the highway certain advanced capitalist nations motor in order to perfect their own consumer-friendly version of totalitarianism. Furthermore, Tater cited the line "Oh, opalescent beauteous waning hopes of peace" as overloaded with "superannuated poetical verbiage" to which Obstreperowski replied, "Oh, waning crystalline benison of publication!" and poured forth further rhapsodic stanzas and plangent lines, redoubling his efforts to disentangle the dead animal from any existing social concern, which was his central and most correctable deviation from Tater and the rest of the New Critical poet/Southern agrarian academics who'd become the poetry establishment after the clearing away of the reds, pinkos, beatniks, African Americans, women, malcontents, homosexuals, disreputables, Comanches, and all so-called undesirables. For all right-thinking, bomb-sheltered, air raid-drilled Americans would know only too well what's at stake: generally speaking, any member of the Legion of Super-Heroes can race at super-speed through the time barrier, whether in a time bubble or under their own power. However, in the *Adventure Comics'* story "The Menace of the Dream Girl," the Time Trapper prevents the heroes from advancing more than thirty days into the future, by dropping what Superboy calls "an iron curtain of time." The rest of the Legion, all residents of the year 2964, understand the metaphor exactly. Ethan Edwards has a grudging respect for the Legion, even though they are no older than his sidekick. He's well aware that aside from

Bouncing Boy and maybe Triplicate Girl, they can take him. But Ronald Reagan is a whole other story (as of yet undepicted in *Adventure Comics*). He has aspirations. He says, "If it's me against Superboy, I got my Red Kryptonite ready. I'll make a monkey outta him, then rat him out as a foreign subversive." Ronald Reagan's connected to a cabal of corporate tycoons and lawyers, underhanded pundits, diabolical economists, and Ku Klux leftovers with a mean streak of conservative *ressentiment*, men who would be revitalizing the Republican Party in just a few years, perhaps around the slogan, "It's time for jumping down from the shelf," and men ornery enough to feel downright disgruntled that Marian Anderson might've once performed an Easter Sunday open-air concert at the Lincoln Memorial, desperate men who've sought out a certain way to prevent such a miscarriage of mellifluence ever again happening, this certain way involving the recruitment of the perfect villain to blow up the aforementioned Memorial and frame J. Robert Oppenheimer, Henry A. Wallace, Pete Seeger and even A. Phillip Randolph. But which villain? Maybe Scar? Or Scarface? Mr. Potter? Reverend Harry Powell? Lex Luthor? The Merry Widow Strangler? Fu Manchu? Auric Goldfinger? Ming the Merciless? Ayn Rand? Captain Bligh? Mrs. Danvers? Cruella de Vil? Snidely Whiplash? Baron Barracuda? "Listen, pard'ners," says Ethan Edwards, "None a them'll do your dirty work for you. They've all lit out for the territories." "Darn," curses—or comes as close as he can to cursing—one ultra-Christian (not a power awesome enough to make membership in the Legion of Super-Heroes) ideologue and future vice-president, sitting alone in the upscale restaurant where ultra-conservative (also not an awesome power) plotters plot because he's not yet married. But before these desperate men can recruit Ethan Edwards, he's off searching space and time for Georgy Girl, dreaming of the someone she could be. And after all these years, the dreams aren't pretty. She could be singing for Motown. "That'd be a pip," complains Ethan. The search continues into the new millennium even though Martin's settled down with Marion Crane's sister (who's looking so much younger and more vivacious now that she's escaped Alfred Hitchcock's clutches, but that's another story, featuring taxidermy, a mother's love, and chocolate syrup down the shower drain), and all Ethan's got left are clues from occasionally published Osborne Obstreperowski poems such as "Hummering With Natalie Wood Through the Small Mammal House." He knows he's on to something, and mumbles, "Come on, Georgy Girl," when he reads the concluding lines, from bush baby point of view, peering out the doorway at one helluva humdinger of an oncoming armored bumper.

The Great American Jesus

Comes to your door all scrubbed and cleaned and cologned in suit and tie like a salesguy out of a car dealership, maybe Chrysler. He's got an American flag pinned to his lapel and an ingenuous smile that literally goes back to the Latin for *native* or *inborn*. Or maybe not only Chrysler, but also Ford, and memorable Ford, like the Model-T. Everything about him says he's got a history and a place in our history, this Caucasian American version, and his cologne smells of musk and almonds. It's just about dusk, and between you and me, something about him is pretty darn sexy. It's understated though, so you almost wouldn't notice. Almost. But, of course, you do and there's the rockets' red glare in his eyes when he introduces himself with that hearty handshake—a real man's handshake, one you can tell is straightforward and honest, right from the heart, like he carries his heart in his hands, and like his heart is the whole wide world. Comes to your door and he's not selling anything; in fact he wants to give you something for free and you can pay for it over time. Which auto company has those commercials about how they're "Like a Rock"? Bob Seger sang that song, a few years after he sang "Ramblin' Gamblin' Man." You never know where somebody's career is going to careen off to. Ted Nugent, for example, started off with the Amboy Dukes singing wacky psychedelia such as "Journey to the Center of the Mind," but ten minutes later he was bow-hunting (deer, bison, boar, and chipmunks) and screeching out "Cat Scratch Fever" all while hanging out at the Trump White House. Or Kenny Rogers.

He also started out psychedelic as all tarnation what with "What Condition My Condition Was In" and ended up as country as a cowpuncher at a Republican convention. Maybe General Motors too. Jesus just seems like the Big Three all in one. And you know he's stayed the course for over two thousand years, with his eyes on America even while they were nailing him to the cross, and the bombs bursting in air, and you almost want to ask if he suffered much, but you know he's not one of those "woe-is-me," feels-sorry-for-himself and makes-excuses-for-being-crucified kind of people. Like America. That's right. On the hand held out for that wholesome handshake, not stigmata but trademark. Comes to your door and you just say the word and you can be on the team and he'll be your captain. And for a moment there you get Bob Seger mixed up with Pete Seeger, but that's absurd because Pete was a red even if he did sing "He Got the Whole World in His Hands." It's like the parable of the lame duck and the dead duck. For the lame duck had a great envy of the dead duck, thinking that the dead duck would enter the house of the Master and be welcome at the Master's table long before the lame duck. And the lame duck sayeth unto the Master, "Why do you place the dead duck before me in your heart?" And the lame duck began hiding in his heart a whole world of thoughts unbecoming to any sort of duck on land or lake. Suddenly, an arrow struck the lame duck through the breast. Fucking Ted Nugent. Can't even let your own personal Jesus have one godforsaken parable about where you end up without it ending up with you. Yes, and the rest of you too. Speaking of which, it's too bad about those automobile corporations losing all kinds of capital and needing financial assistance from American taxpayers.

The banks too. Which are made of marble. With a guard at every door. Comes to your door and you just say the word and fess up. Don't you long to belong to every gathering of more than three in his name using him as their personal enabler for whatever righteous self-centering enters their brain, and I'd swear the cologne's got a hint of bitter almonds, but what a handshake! The kind that'd send you scooting down the gulley and over to grandma's house for a piece of apple pie. A real miracle of a handshake. Something they'd mention a time or two among the descending red, white, and blue balloons at any given Republican convention. Did you confuse the *logos* with the logos on his palms? And something about a red glare and the parable of the lame nation and the reanimated nation (made great again) and incorporation after incorporation that seems to go back all the way to the Latin for *embodied* from *corpus* meaning *body* and the haughty host in triumph and a wolf draped in Old Glory and the vaults are stuffed with silver and the sweat that we have sweated and the wreck on the highway and the love taken to town and the handshake instead of a kiss and he's going next door to see your neighbor and it feels like he's leaving for another country, like he'll soon be at home in another nation, and we want to stop him, to ask why he prefers our neighbor to ourselves, we want to say, "O Jesus! For God's sake, turn around."

Toward Smart-Ass Proletarian Poetry

Jeepers and criminy! What happened to all the manifestoes??! Seems like last century you couldn't turn around without bumping into a poetical manifesto of some major aesthetico-socio–political importance. (Oops!! I believe I forgot *ecomomico*-; that's okay, those manifestoes mostly did too.) I recall in high school, the toilet stalls were supplied with that institutional toilet paper that's dispensed in single sheets, and half of the time you'd pull out one little sheet and what few single sheets remained would slide out onto the wet or damp or otherwise disheartening floor (but don't think about whatever image is now manifesting itself in your imagination; think thoughts poetical). Some of the students substituted the school newspaper (possibly an oblique comment on students' right to freedom of the press, or perhaps a manifestation of school spirit), but there was always (or an oblique remark concerning students' rights to freedom of speech and expression) some Marinetti screed or *Blast* pronouncement that would work just as well—kinda right wing but serviceable. And by the way, what about all the artsy old lefties? Okay, maybe "art as a weapon" was not enough of a guarantee to keep Stalin from signing that pact with Hitler, and those had to be hard times for poets, what with having to choose between Uncle Joe and Uncle Ezra (and his squawking Possum), and then there was all that televised folderol with Eugene McCarthy fulminating and fumfurting around while poets hid most of their politics in proverbial or pre-verbal closets, or under the bed with their back issues of *Masses, New Masses* and *The Rebel Poet*, while dead animal poetry became so ubiquitous as to be symbolic of some several dysfunctions of the state and civil society that could not be named—a great white whale in the living room, so to speak. Bad time in the U.S. to be a deer or squirrel or chipmunk or porcupine or armadillo or woodchuck or toad or turtle. (Bad time to be a skunk too, but that was the nocturnal stalkings of Robert Lowell. Naked. On an equestrian statue.) So the question now is as follows: should one be crafting a poetry that is smart-ass proletarian or is one a smart ass crafting proletarian poetry? And didn't Kenneth Fearing get where they got years before the New York Poets got where they got—and in New York, too? Speaking of New York, I arrived there right after "FORD TO CITY: DROP DEAD." As to the breath, one does most likely need to be breathing in order to read this stuff. Maybe even to write it. While we conceive the most democratic of poetries, there nevertheless are some minimal requirements. After all, even a broad-based working-class organization would require a general adherence to certain ideas, payment of dues, and perhaps work with the organization (or one of its many front groups). Even Frank O'Hara demands we eat our mashed potatoes. (No, he doesn't.) Not that I'm complaining—I love mashed potatoes—maybe a little olive oil and garlic. (No, it's just the opposite; he's complaining that some poets act like, "You have to eat your meat and potatoes with these drippings, which are tears—and rhythm, assonance, and all that stuff.") Well, he never disparaged French Fries. That was the Republican Party, and later. Oh, and Brussels sprouts! Fry them up in olive oil with some garlic, leek, and jalapeno—words cannot describe. (But did O'Hara have anything to say about keeping your parenthetical and outside-paren voices straight? Ha! Not likely.) I'll take over from here: Yet not the worst time to be an old fish with five broken off pieces of line hanging from your lip—"or four and a wire leader/ with the swivel still attached"—that's the kind of animal that survives poems and lives to swim another day, which reminds me of a line a friend and comrade once wrote in an internal document about the mass movement being the sea in which we little red fishes swim. (That was Jim, and he sorta semi-lifted that from Mao Zedong, but we didn't care, we were some groovy kinda anarcho-Trotskyists who labeled the Soviet Union *and* China "state capitalist" and peeved all the more traditional Trotskyists—and Maoists and Stalinists to boot—and let me tell you, Stalin owned boots. And besides, the left was where I learned the first principle of poetry: Language is communal, so if it's a good line, lift it.) But a coupla social context kinda things you need to know for your aesthetical endeavors: the bad racist days are always supposedly in the past, and the most recent method of executing death row prisoners is always supposedly more humane. New and improved! Nitrogen gas! Whiter whites!! Or is one a smart-ass proletarian just writing some wackadoodle poems? Negative capability or not? Langston Hughes to Theodor Adorno:

How do you make a poem
        from nothing
                may exist
                        which is not like
        the world
as it is? But then I am reminded of the Anti-Christ of manifestoes, The Powell Memo. Written in smoke-filled shadows and distributed

on the sly by Lewis Powell, a sleazy corporate lawyer who litigated on behalf of tobacco companies and the Tobacco Institute (a cancer-promoting trade group sponsoring slimy lobbyists, creepy advertisers, fake scientists, and at least one fraudulent journalist, all advocating unrestricted smoking until their scam was stubbed out by the Surgeon General), and served as sleazy Chairman of the Richmond School Board while said whiter-white bunch were numbered among the "massive resistance" to *Brown v. Board of Education*, and who went on to be a sleazy Supreme Court justice, paving the way (by helping decide that money is speech and corporations have First Amendment rights) to the 2010 *Citizen's United* decision. New York in the mid-'70s: layoffs of teachers, firefighters, and police; hospital closures; tuition instituted at city colleges; Ford and Carter denying aid; and the banker/werewolf/vampire/mummy/clowns bellowing out, "Down here they all default!" Could we have used a socio-politico-economico-poetical manifesto? You betcha! We might've been smart-ass and poetic and all, but we just weren't manifesting. Problem was, no mass movement as we approached the Reagan eighties and Clinton nineties. Right-wing Christians get into politics and keep voting for the candidate who most resembles the Anti-Christ. New Democrats new sentencing and sentencing: "Super-predators! Coming to an urban location near you!" Turn of the stomach of the century Bush years. Before you know it, economic inequality, unemployment, war mongering, and mass incarceration are up; unions, social safety nets, and generosity of spirit are down. What with Trump & Klan these days, those Christains are very close to getting what they voted for. And, yes, thanks to Betsy DeVos, there's no such thing as a free lunch, not in public school. To say, "You can't fight city hall" at this point would be a cliché and should be avoided in smart-ass poetry. (Besides, "it is right to rebel.") (Yes, that was lifted from Mao Zedong.) Same goes for "Only in America." (No, not that it's lifted from Mao, but that it's a cliché. Besides, it also has political problems because the US is only a part, but not the solution—at all. It should be *Not only, but also in America.*) Hence, certain ideas held by a political organization (and its individual members) could be called one's *line*, as in *party line* or "What is your organization's *line* on the Soviet Union, and why don't you think it is a degenerated workers' state, and how can you call yourself a Trotskyist if you don't, given Trotsky himself coined the term in *The Revolution Betrayed?*" So, you see, the party line leads us right to the poetic line, for even

                after allowing for Stalin, his henchmen, their hangers-on,

                     their progeny and apologists, and their
        ilk, epigones, petty bureaucrats, lackies, stooges,
             further hangers-on, there just weren't enough
                degenerates to degenerate the Soviet Union.
That's why
        Stalin needed the show trials, the executions, famine
            from above, the Gulag, more show trials—Oh, and
        revisionists
             (never forget your revisionists nor your
             revisions
even though Allen Ginsberg was all: "First thought, best thought." [Yeah, right, tell it to Hegel]). Speaking of revisioning, that was the

project of my all-male high school—we'd be pegged and repackaged along one of three paths: college-bound, military-bound (that'd be ROTC), or factory-bound (including your choice of three of the following: electric shop, woodworking shop, foundry shop, auto shop, and the foul rag and bone shop—in which we'd learn about mixed and mashed metaphors and post-millennial alliteration, maybe allusion as well). Oops, I believe I forgot to mention that Ezra Pound probably could craft an aesthetico-economic manifesto, but it would also be, well, phallocentric, Pound being a dick and all. (Hmmm, *Dick and All* sounds like Ezra's answer to William Carlos Williams.) Okay then, first principles: No ideas but in things and in left-wing political ideas—because, quite frankly, things are a fucking mess: privatization, union-busting, austerity programs, deregulation, structural racism, lethal injection, implicit bias, mass incarceration, exorbitant and mediocre healthcare, racial profiling, high taxes on earnings, low taxes on inheritance, no taxes on corporations, strategic racism, defunded education, charter schools, individual freedoms for the wealthy, individual responsibility for everyone else, attacks on women's rights, gay rights, trans rights, blanket denial of immigrant rights, but the Klan has the right to free speech?

> This land is
> > your land but the
> banks are made
> > > of marble this land
> is my land with
> > a guard at every
> door from California to the New York

highlands and the vaults

are stuffed from

the redwood forests with

silver to the Gulf Stream

waters that we have

sweated for this

land is made

for you might could kick the commies out of the trade unions, or the commie trade unions out of the AFL–CIO, but you won't kick the libertarian billionaires and their lackeys and stooges and ilk and progeny out of the Republican Party: *Invasion of the Body Snatchers.* That's thanks to the Powell Memo, aka The Powell Memorandum, aka The Powell (jeepers and criminy!) Manifesto. It's a basic problem/solution essay-type structure with the evils of the '60s (democracy, equality, anti–imperialism, social justice) being the problem and capitalists and their apologists being the solution. Problem? "A recent poll of students on 12 representative campuses reported that: 'Almost half the students favored socialization of basic U.S. industries.'" The persons perusing this m-m-memo at their local Chamber of Commerce are already hiding under their reading tables. Problem? Ralph N-N-Nader!!!—"was paid a lecture fee of $2,500 for 'denouncing America's big corporations in venomous language . . . bringing (rousing and spontaneous) bursts of applause' when he was asked when he planned to run for President," and, "He thinks, and says quite bluntly, that a great many corporate executives belong in prison." P-P-Prison?!! The big boys around the Tobacco Institute's conference table are pulling out their hair (or scratching their bald spots) and gnashing their teeth and pinching their neighbor and guzzling gin. Elsewheres, the traditional Trotskyists go blue in face while raving, "The workers are not degenerates; the bureaucrats are." What about *eroded* workers' state? "But how could a workers' state erode?" *Erasured workers' state?* "What? The *workers* in *workers' state* held under erasure? That's just deconstructive folderol." Well, that pretty much describes the Stalin years: workers erasured. "Whither the degenerated workers' state?" It's like the old joke: did you take a shower today? No, why, is one missing? How many years did it take me to catch on to that one? But the Traditional Trotskyists never did. For them it was: nationalization + planned economy=socialism. Oh, yeah, one's missing. Heh-heh. I get it now, Grandma. From Robert Frost to Louis Althusser: "Something there is that doesn't love a state ideological apparatus": (Whose woods these are I think I know--/ Some old New England capitalist's/ He doesn't scare me any though/ For I'm a communist!!//These woods are quaint, but I'll be gone/For I have theses to write upon/ And years of therapy with Lacan/ And years of therapy with Lacan.) When will we, in our epoch of neoliberal post-globalized re-imperialist always-already-in-decay, catch on? Sometimes you feel like Wallace Stevens waltzing through "*Esthétique du Mal*" until Canto XIV when, attempting to make the anarcho-communist Victor Serge sound like he's criticizing the Soviet Union circa 1920 from the right, the poet trips over his own supreme fiction. You can try to stick with poetry that'll make nothing happen, but from Auden to eternity, poetry's a happening thing! Anyway, first principles: while bourgeois art appreciation and fugitive New Critics may have constructed an aesthetico-ethical hierarchy of humor to go along with the socioeconomic ones of class and race, not to mention the similarly oppressive ones of gender and gender orientation—Oh, which reminds me to credit Tennessee Williams for penning the great postwar protest play in a time when playwrights, novelists, poets, musicians, intellectuals, and the working class(!) weren't supposed to protest in literature (or anywhere else!) anymore— that'd be *A Streetcar Named Desire*, which argues (OMG!! scream the fugitives and appreciators, ART DOESN'T ARGUE!! Taxi! Taxi! Take us to a dead sparrow poem, and step on it!!)—as I was saying, argues a society that oppresses gay people oppresses women and eventually everyone else but for those who can be organized to "hang back with the brutes"—you know, Nazis and neo-Nazis and alt-right clowns and neoliberal totalitarians—Where was I? Problem? Holy crap! Our elite universities: "Yale, like every other major college, is graduating scores of bright young men who are practitioners of 'the politics of despair.' These young men despise the American political and economic system . . . (their) minds seem to be wholly closed." And university presidents are smacking themselves upside the head and wearing their dirty laundry in public. Problem? We want Our Money!!! "Favorite current targets are proposals for tax incentives through changes in depreciation rates and investment credits. These are usually described in the media as 'tax breaks,' 'loop holes' or 'tax benefits' for the benefit of business. As viewed by a columnist in the *Post,* such tax measures would benefit 'only the rich, the owners of big companies.'" Now the captains of industry and movers and shakers of political, business, and civic life are ready for the call to arms! And call to arms it is: "[Powell's] overall tone was doomsday and militant.

Referring to the enemies that Powell said were arrayed against the Chamber [of Commerce]— largely on campuses, in the media and in the courts — he used the term *attack* 18 times; *revolt / revolution / revolutionaries* five; *war/ warfare* four; *assault* four; *hostility* two; *destruction* two; and *shotgun attack* and *rifle shot* one each. The stakes, he said, were tantamount to life and death." "Oh, whattodo? Whattodo?" cried the slimy elite. "Where was I?" Ah, yes, humor for smart-ass proletarian poetry is an open field: anecdotal, blue, burlesque, gallows, deadpan, droll, epigrammatic, cosmic, farcical, fractured, fragmented, deadpan gallows, highbrow, lowbrow, hyperbolic, lowperbolic, middlebrowberbolic, gallows burlesque, lyrical, ironic, linguistic, mordant, morbid, parodic, juvenile, penile, anti-coagulant, troll-like, crocodile burlesque, tragicomical, melodic, metaphorical, metaphysical, episodic, meta-poetical, mumbled, fumbled, anti-psychotic, economico-tragicomical, anti-fascist, rhetorical, risqué, satirical, screwball, self-deprecating, self-referential, anti-presidential, T Rex tragicomical, anti-neoliberal, situational, symbolical, scatological, slapstick, surreal, way left-wing political, and didn't Kenneth Fearing get where they got years before the New York Poets got where they—(Waitaminute! Didn't the New York poets get there almost before you were begotten? And weren't you in NYC only about two-and-a-half years? And not publishing a manifesto or even poetry anyways but working on a lefty newspaper?) What the heck's the matter with left-wing journalism? Meanwhile, one's line

      on the nature of the Soviet Union matters because

    one's vision matters

of human freedom, no second rate

                                    state–capitalism masquerading as
                    "socialist," no democratic façade for
totalitarians a fine (line/ by line)

                                                break with capital
                    (of the free/ verse poem) for
          property is theft;

                              poverty is violence
and irony   (satire) may be   our most important
product (/weapon)

as when Beverly comes home from a teachers' union conference
with a United Steelworkers Union T-shirt that says on the front
TOUGH ENOUGH and STEELWORKER FOREVER on
the back, and being a smart-ass proletarian poet (or a smart-ass
writing proletarian poetry) manifesting, I consider how the United
Steelworkers Union went for the Experimental Negotiating
Agreement (ENA) in the mid '70s through the '80s, guaranteeing
raises per contract negotiation so that the union would give up
the right to strike, and then the owners claimed wages were too
high, shut down plants, laid off tons of workers, diversified their
portfolios, and ended steel production in the US as we knew it.
(And speaking of dicks and all, do you ever wish your pajamas
featured little cartoon phallo-figures of Ezra Pound and T.S. Eliot?)
So I think of wearing that T-shirt with that particular slogan on the
back, and then I think of me myself wearing that particular T-shirt,
and, "TOUGH ENOUGH"—and is that world-class working-
class irony or what? But a coupla social context kinda things
you need to know for your aesthetical endeavors: the Fugitives
begat from the foam of their close reading the New Criticism

from the headache of which fully formed and armored came an apolitical Virginia Woolf apolitical Jean Toomer apolitical Samuel Beckett apolitical Elizabeth Bishop apolitical James Joyce apolitical Edith Wharton apolitical (oh, and straight!) Harlem Renaissance apolitical New Negro apolitical Surrealism the apolitical Emily Dickinson before the garrulous Walt Whitman and the grievously mistaken left-wing poets, playwrights, and fictioneers. Difficult but not impossible to write poetry with fiction ears. How do you stop a bad guy with a gun? Keep big money out of elections. Why did the chicken cross the road? To get away from Tyson Foods, "innovators uniquely positioned to reshape what it means to feed our world" by creating one big Gulf of Mexico dead zone (that'd be *hypoxic* or "low-oxygen" areas) where marine life either leaves or dies. This is how we know freedom of choice is perfectly natural. As with the undocumented folks from Honduras or Guatemala or El Salvador or Syria. Of course, so is the 1%'s exacerbation of the 99%'s exasperation. Oh, yes, Powell had a strategy: Go forth, my flying monkeys of capital! My Friedmans and Hayeks and Buchanans! (O, my!!) Bombard the universities with business graduate programs, phony baloney about faculty balance, and free speech for neoliberal creeps and alt-right white supremacists! Go forth and monitor TV and radio, journals and books, and complain complain complain, call them "liberal media" lips curled with disdain! "Fake news!" Cook up Dinesh D'Souza, Ann Coulter and Rush Limbaugh! Go forth and build sensible deprivation think tanks! Oh, and think deep thoughts! Deny climate change! Claim intelligence a racial characteristic! Claim women want to have babies before they're old-maid defense lawyers or college professors! Go forth, my Reagans and Bushes! My Clintons!! Claim pre-emptive war is a novel idea! That unemployment, disease, prison, obesity, and addiction are matters of individual responsibility! Oh, and claim the more of the nation's wealth that goes to the wealthy, the more will trickle down—like from that faucet that your landlord won't fix because he's out spending your hard-earned money on sex toys! Go forth, hie thee to the law schools and hie thee to the courts! Bring forth a new generation to twist the Constitution and torture logic until corporations are people whiter than white; money is speech; the death penalty isn't racist, it's just used on Black people; and soon, yes, very soon, abortion is murder. Go forth and privatize, privatize, privatize—the schools, the prisons, the army, state governments, local governments. Turn parks into malls and citizens into shoppers! Lower corporate taxes! Free trade! Go forth, my flying monkeys of capital, and bring forth a multitude of lobbyists to write the bills for the congressmen. Lead the congressmen from the temptations of consumers' rights and deliver them from the evils of environmental legislation. Go forth on monkey wings and create the American Legislative Exchange Council (ALEC!) to produce model bills for state and federal governments, weakening unions and opposing gun control! Lighten up those environmental regulations and come down hard on undocumented workers! Deregulate the banks and deep freeze corporate taxes! Debliterate inheritance taxes! Turn those public schools to charters! Turn those voters away with tougher and more tougher ID laws! Oh, now and forever, before Armageddon is upon us, We Want Our Money!!! We all defraud!! We all defraud down here!!! And did I mention Lewis Powell's pivotal role in the reinstitution of the death penalty? Takes me back to New York 1977: the lights go out all over the city, and the people repay the bankers and the government for austerity with hours of liberating wannabe-commodities from all kinds of stores. Makes one wonder how the people of the US will reward the ruling elite for the economic slippery slope down from Reagan's rise to Trump's untruths, falsehoods, fibs, exaggerations (the most well-attended Inauguration *ever*), fictions, lies, deceptions ("No collusion!"), tall tales, fabrications (right out of the Stalinist School of), whoppers ("I am the least racist person . . ."), and lies and lies and bald-faced tweets ("Not now, Melania, I'm twitting" "I'll say, and *as if*" "Aw, c'mon, Melania! The pee-pee tape is fake news!") fulminationizing "Crooked Hillary," "Witch Hunt," "Cheatin' Obama," "Fake News CNN," "MS-13 Lover Nancy Pelosi," Iran, DACA, "Little Rocket Man," "chain migration," "the Failing *New York Times*," "Sour [Don] Lemon," "Sloppy Michael Moore," "Pocahontas," "Liberal Fake News NBC," "Disgraced and discredited Bob Mueller and his Angry Democrat Thugs," "FBI Lover Boy" Peter Strzok, "SOB" Black NFL players, etcetera, "Low-IQ Maxine Waters," etcetera, "Wacky Omarosa," etcetera, etcetera. And the Russian prostitutes sing, "O, say can you see/ Where pervy Trump had us pee? . . ." (Lists are also great for poetry. Nothing's more listless than a listless poem.) Meanwhile, back at the Axis of Evil, it's Saudi Arabia, Israel, and USA. (I'd better take over from here. The mashed potatoes, are they in or out? Ah heck, what's next? Maybe Mina Loy pajamas whereon she's depicted leading us past Marinetti and Pound and a shitload of corporate executives and past presidents and other sleazy politicians and [Lewis!] justices, through the Inferno and up into Purgatory where we can catch our breath and pray for a better world and conceive the most democratic of poetries, remembering to always, always go for the joke at the expense of capital, for soon it'll be fracking in those Gulf Stream waters, and any poisonous chemicals and oil spills and meat industry toxins from manure and fertilizer will all be "externalities"—meaning the oil and meat companies won't pick up the tab or clean up after

rainbow rainbow rainbow

And I let myself go, "Jeepers! This

is a cry for help from

nation and nature itself

for the nurture of

smart-ass proletarian poetry!"

)

Notes

Cover —Walter Benjamin's quote is from "Paralipomena to 'On the Concept of History'" in *Selected Writings, Volume 4: 1938-1940*, edited by Howard Eiland and Michael W. Jennings. (Belknap Press 2003). I came to it by way of Michael Löwy's, *Fire Alarm: Reading Walter Benjamin's 'On the Concept of History'* NY:Verso, 2005.

Resurrection of the Great American Elegy—H.P. Lovecraft.

How Economics Became a Discipline—Michael Powell's 6 June 2009 article in the *New York Times*, "Bank Accused of Pushing Mortgage Deals on Blacks," includes the following information regarding the Baltimore branch of Wells Fargo: "Another loan officer stated in an affidavit filed last week that employees had referred to blacks as 'mud people' and to subprime lending as 'ghetto loans.'" For the story of the CIA/Contra sale of crack cocaine to the Crips and Bloods, see Ryan Grim's *This Is Your Country on Drugs: The Secret History of Getting High in America* and also Alexander Cockburn and David St. Clair's *Whiteout: The CIA, Drugs and the Press*.

Don't Vote, Vomit—Lynne McTaggart's *The Intention Experiment: Using Your Thoughts to Change Your Life and the World*.

Sputnik and the Russian Bear —Masha Vorontsova appears in Luke Harding's "Russian Bears Treat Graveyards as 'Giant Refrigerators'" in *The Guardian* 26 Oct. 2010.

Rifle Out the Sixth Floor Window—Quotation concerning "intra-administration division" in Stanza three is from Peter Dale Scott's *Deep Politics and the Death of JFK*. Quotation on Oswald in stanza three from the Warren Commission Report as quoted by Gaeton Fonzi in *The Last Investigation*. Other sources include James W. Douglas, *JFK and the Unspeakable: Why He Died and Why it Matters*; David Talbot, *Brothers: The Hidden History of the Kennedy Years*; Larry Hancock, *Someone Would Have Talked:*

The Assassination of President John F. Kennedy and the Conspiracy to Mislead History; Seymour Hersh, *The Dark Side of Camelot.*

Is This a Bad Time?—For quotation regarding damage done by the Koch brothers, see Pam Martens' "Koch Industries Is Staffing Up With Voter Data Scientists to Tip The November Election to the Extreme Right" in *Counterpunch* 23 July 2018. The visit to a plantation house, the story of the bathing of the slavers, and the question about seeing the slave quarters all actually happened about thirty years ago. Helpful sources include Kathleen Belew, *Bring the War Home;* Linda Gordon, *The Second Coming of the KKK;* Bushart, Craig, and Barnes, *Soldiers of God:White Supremacists and Their Holy War for America;* Alexander Reid Ross, *Against the Fascist Creep;* David Niewart, *Alt America: The Rise of the Radical Right in the Age of Trump;* Matthew N. Lyons, *Insurgent Supremacists:The US Far Right's Challenge to State and Empire.;* Seth Hettena, *Trump/Russia: A Definitive History;* Rhoda Rae Gutierrez, "Beating the Neoliberal Blame Game: Teacher and Parent Solidarity and the 2012 Chicago Teachers' Strike," *Monthly Review,* June 2013. Also helpful were news items on red-state teachers' strikes, confederate statues, gun control, Trump and white supremacy, Supreme Court rulings, the Malhuer National Forest stand-off, and Trump administration goings-on in *Democracy Now!, The Intercept, Counterpunch, Vox, Vice, The Nation* and other news sources.

"Stone Free"?—Baruch Spinoza

Orgone Accumulator—Myron Sharaf, *Fury on Earth:A Biography of Wilhelm Reich.* Wilhelm Reich's *Sex-Pol: Essays 1929-1934; Listen, Little Man;The Mass Psychology of Fascism.* E. Fuller Torrey, *The Roots of Treason: Ezra Pound and the Secret of St. Elizabeth's.* Various websites concerning Wilhelm Reich and orgone were also helpful.

"Straw Bales" and **"Just Like Volume Two"** are responses to Mike Barrett's *Recto Verso, volumes 1* and 2, (respectively) both read in manuscript.

Certain Proclivities—James Whale's *The Bride of Frankenstein* (1935) is essential viewing. Other influences include David J. Skal, *The Monster Show: A Cultural History of* Horror; E. Fuller Torrey, *The Roots of Treason: Ezra Pound and the Secret of St. Elizabeth's;* C. David Heymann, *Ezra Pound: The Last Rower.*

Search Me, Little Varmints—We take as our text John Ford (dir.) *The Searchers* (1956). The Seekers song, "Georgy Girl" (1966) is also an influence. The Legion of Super-Heroes story titled "The Menace of the Dream Girl" first appeared in *Adventure Comics*, v. 1 # 317, in the February, 1964, issue. John Frederick Nims (ed.) *Western Wind*, 2nd edition was also a great help.

Toward Smart-Ass Proletarian Poetry—All quotations after the recurring word: *Problem?* Are from the Powell Memo. The poem also features lines from Frank O'Hara, Elizabeth Bishop, Tennessee Williams, Langston Hughes, and Theodor Adorno. Quotation from Steven Higg's "A Call to Arms in the Class War: From the Top Down" from *CounterPunch* 11 May 2012 begins "[Powell's] overall tone . . . . " Helpful books include: Naomi Klein, *The Shock Doctrine*; Michelle Alexander, *The New Jim Crow*; Ian Haney Lopez, *Dog Whistle Politics*; Kim Philips-Fein, *Fear City*: Matt Taibbi, *Griftopia*, Nancy MacLean, *Democracy in Chains;* Peter Mirowski's *Never Let a Serious Crisis Go To Waste*, and several other books by David Harvey, Noam Chomsky, Wayne Price, Klein and Taibbi.

Other sources include Wikipedia and various websites, films, music, and other entertainment commodities and media.

Acknowledgments

Everything I write and am is for **Beverly Stewart**. We have been enjoying The Grateful Factor since 4 November 1994 (First date—Thai food and *The Shawshank Redemption*). Grateful I am.

With thanks to . . . All who helped make specific poems in this collection happen, including: Friend and fellow Cthulhuville dissident **Robert Wayner** and his late dog **Abby** • **Amy England** who provoked my foray into Surrealist poetry • My mother, **Louise Rogaczewski** and **Karen and Bill Couch**. Also my niece, **Laurie Couch,** for volunteering to be digested by a bear or three after her decease. And their little dog, too—a.k.a. **Sputnik** • My late brother-in-law **Dean Elkins** who got me started on "'Stone Free'?" • **Mike Barrett**, for our friendship and for his elegant and intelligent poetry • **Julie Lindquist** for reading an earlier, not quite as smart-ass version of the "Toward a Smart-Ass Proletarian Poetry"• Fellow poet and friend **Beatriz Badikian-Gartler** for inviting me to read with her and poet/friends **Ixtaccihuatl Menchaca** and **Elizabeth Marino** at the Uptown Arts Center (March 2018) an event which helped inspire "Armed Teachers [With Mental Illness]" • Fellow Rothko fans **Susan Alcorn** and **Gwynne Gertz** • Fellow horror fans **Sandy Schulze-Mosley, Jeremy and Jennifer Balek, Angela Alsterda, Sabrina Schulze-Alsterda** (and again the Couch family, and my mother) • My comrades and friends on the left, including members of **Students for a Democratic Society** and of the **Revolutionary Socialist League,** especially **Bruce Gottfried, Susan Alcorn,** and **Ian Scott Horst** • **Brooke Bergan** for setting up the 10 a Day group on Facebook, and all of the participants, including **Anne Flanagan, Mike Barrett, Michael Settles II, Diane Prokop, Ann Lammas, David Andres,** and **John Petroshius** • **Steve Tomasula** and the &NOW Festival 2018 at Notre Dame University for facilitating my lovely October 6 reading • **Joe Fedorko, Jen Wilson,** and the **Roosevelt Adjunct**

Faculty Association for inviting me to read at the November 8 meeting • Therapist extraordinaire, **Ida Roldán** • *American Letters & Commentary*, to wit **David Ray Vance** (Editor and Chief) for culling, arranging, editing, designing and publishing, and **Teagan Downey** (Editorial Intern) and **Christopher Guzman** (Associate Editor) for their keen editorial assistance

Plus . . . All the friends, peers, writers, and dears who kept me reading and thinking and prevented me from becoming a pod person while constructing the poems: **Bruce Gottfried, Susan Alcorn, Carin Perkins, Anne Flanagan, Brooke Bergan, Mike Barrett, Lea Graham, Julie Lindquist, Ixtaccihuatl Menchaca, Barbara Hill, Gwynne Gertz, David Jolliffe, Rachel Srubas, Michael J. Perkovich, Karen Halvorsen Schreck, Jeffery Renard Allen, Beatriz Badikian-Gartler, Cynthia Davidson, Beth Franken, Linda Vavra, Joseph Fedorko, Jennifer Langdon, Patti Renda, Rashmi Varma, Michael Anania, Imani Bolling, Kitty Shanahan, Giles Kotcher, Bernadette Ostrozovich, Robert Archambeau, Eckhard Gerdes, Anna Stotts, Trudy Lewis, Kim Franz, John Kimsey, Carol Mahan Kimsey, Ian Scott Horst, LuAnn Swartzlander, Kian Bergstrom, Elizabeth Marino, Kim Franz, Patrick Garrett, Mark Magoon, Connor Bernhard, Jennifer Barthel, Joy Jaeger, Garth Lewis, David Ray Vance, Robert Wayner** and **Babie Pillow**

And obvioiusly . . . My family: mother **Louise Rogaczewski,** sisters, **Karen Couch** and **Kathy Elkins**, brother (in-law) **Bill Couch**, cousins **Tom Schulze** and **Sandy Schulze-Mosley,** and adult nieces and nephews, in-laws and outlaws, including **Laurie Couch, Bobby Couch, Casey Murphy, Sabrina Schulze-Alsterda and Bryan, Angela Alsterda and Dre, Jeremy and Jennifer Balek**, **Kris Schulze and Lisa Schulze**, Juvenile delinquent cats, **Gertrude** and **Virginia** (b. July, 2017), and our wonderful dogs, **Sammy** (1995-May 22, 2010), **Jasmine** (2001- July 9, 2017) and **Seamus** (b.April 2010)

About the Author

Frank Rogaczewski holds a Ph.D. in Literature and Creative Writing from the University of Illinois at Chicago and teaches at Roosevelt University in Chicago. His first book, *The Fate of Humanity in Verse* was published by AL&C in 2009. He lives in Berwyn with his wife Beverly Stewart.

About the Publisher

American Letters & Commentary, Inc., is an independent not-for-profit corporation 501(c)3. For over twenty years AL&C was dedicated to publishing a literary annual promoting innovative and "difficult" writing, a tradition it now carries on by way of this book imprint. We are grateful to the English Department and The College of Liberal and Fine Arts for their support. The views expressed in this book are not necessarily those of UTSA, its administration, its employees, or its students, nor are they necessarily the views of AL&C's editors, its volunteers, or its donors.

www.ingramcontent.com/pod-product-compliance
Lightning Source LLC
Chambersburg PA
CBHW051734090426
42738CB00010B/2257